LINUX

ADMINISTRATION

The Simple and Powerful Guide to
Master Linux Administration

DAVID A. WILLIAMS

TABLE OF CONTENTS

Introduction

This book, *'Linux Administration - The Simple and Powerful Guide to Master Linux Administration'* is the second book in our series of books on Linux System Administration.

In the first book, we went through the basics of a Linux operating system and the essential functions that a system administrator should be capable of performing. In this book, things will get a little more serious, and we will deep dive into tasks that a system administrator is expected to perform at the server level and the hardware level. We learned how to install the Red Hat Enterprise Linux operating system in the first book.

A manual installation makes sense if you have only a single system on which you need to install the operating system. But when you are working as a system admin at a big organization, there are hundreds and thousands of systems on which you will need to install a Linux operating system, and doing so manually, one by one will exhaust you. Therefore, in this book, we start with learning about Kickstart, which is an automated installer to help you install the Red Hat Enterprise Linux on multiple systems using a configuration file.

We learned about grep and vim in the first book, but we will be taking a deeper dive with them in this second book in our Linux Administration series. We will learn in brief about automation using Linux operating systems using a tool known as cron. We will look at the security aspects of Linux through the concepts of Access Control Lists and SELinux security.

We learned how to create local users in our first book, and we will look at creating network-level users in this book. We will also work on hard disks, creating partitions, and creating logical volumes in this book. We will conclude this book by studying about the boot process of Red Hat Enterprise Linux 7 and learning how to tackle issues faced in the boot process.

CHAPTER 1

Using Kickstart to Automate Red Hat Enterprise Linux Installations

We already know that Linux is one of the most powerful operating systems available to us today. Almost every server in the world today, be it by a cloud giant like Amazon Web Services or a smaller provider like GoDaddy, is powered by the Linux operating system. Linux is preferred over other operating systems such as MAC and Windows because it is open source and highly customizable. The following features of Linux make it a highly desirable operating system by every organization.

- Portability: Linux is a very portable operating system, which supports all kinds of hardware available today.

- Open Source: Linux was developed as a community project, and its code is still freely available even today.

- Multi-user: Linux supports the creation and management of multiple users on the operating system.

- Shell: An interpreter program known as the bash shell is available in Linux from where you can give instructions to the operating system via command line.

- File System Hierarchy: There is a standard in which files are maintained and classified on Linux.

- Security: There are features like authentication and access control lists, which make Linux a very secure operating system.

In this chapter, we will learn how we can automate installations for Red Hat Enterprise Linux using something known as a kickstart. The objective of this chapter is to understand the concepts and architecture of kickstart. We will also try to understand the kickstart configuration file available in Red Hat Enterprise Linux. By the end of this chapter, you will be able to identify the key configuration elements available inside the configuration file for kickstart.

A Throwback to Manual Installation

Before we start with the automated process of installing Red Hat Enterprise Linux, let us quickly revise through the manual installation process. The point of this activity is to know the parameters that we had to input for the manual installation so that you can compare them with the parameters passed during the automated installation.

Installing Red Hat Enterprise Linux 7

There are various options for installing Red Hat Enterprise Linux 7, but the steps we have provided in this section will help you install Red Hat Enterprise Linux 7 with minimal software and no graphical interface. You do not need to panic because of the absence of a graphical interface, as most tasks that need to be performed as a Linux System Administrator are done using the command line.

As we have seen in the first book of this series, you would have a USB drive in which you would have created boot media for the Red

Hat Enterprise Linux installation. After booting up the USB, you would follow the process given below.

1. Plug the USB drive into your computer's USB port and start your computer. You should make sure that you have enabled USB boot in your computer's BIOS settings

2. Once the computer boots up, you should be able to see a list of bootable devices and one of them would be your USB drive titled Red Hat Enterprise Linux 7

3. Once the system is up, you will get an option to choose your language. Click on Continue after you have selected the required language

4. You will now be presented with the Installation Summary screen, where you can customize the installation of Red Hat Enterprise Linux 7 as per your needs. Select the Date and Time to configure the locale for your system using the world map that is provided and then click on Done

5. On the next screen, choose the language for your system and your keyboard. We would recommend that you use the English language

6. The installation source for your Red Hat Enterprise Linux 7 will be the USB drive primarily. Still, you can add other sources for the repositories by specifying locations on the internet on your local network using protocols such as FTP, HTTP, HTTPS, etc. Once you have defined all your sources, click on Done. You can leave it on the default source if you do not have any other sources to be used

7. Now, you can select the software that has to be installed along with the operating system. As we have discussed, we will only be installing essential software. To do this, select on

Minimal Install along with Compatibility Libraries Add-ons and click on Done

8. On the next step, we will configure partitions for the system. Click Installation Destination and then choose the LVM scheme for partition. This will allow you to manage the disk space. Now, click on "Click here to create them automatically."

9. You will be presented with the default partition scheme, which you can edit as per your requirements. As we are going to use the Red Hat Enterprise Linux 7 operating system to learn server administration, you can use the essential partition scheme as given below

/boot partition which should have disk space of 500 MB and should be a non-LVM partition

/root partition with a minimum disk space of 20 GB and an LVM partition

/home partition which should be an LVM partition

/var partition with a minimum disk space of 20 GB and an LVM partition

The filesystem that you need to use is XFS, which is the world's most advanced filesystem right now. Once you have specified the edits for the partitions, click on Update Settings and then click Done followed by Accept Changes, which will apply your edits to the system.

10. This is the final step before initiating the Red Hat Enterprise Linux 7 installation. You need to set up the network. Select "Network and Hostname," which will allow you to specify a hostname for your system. You can use a short hostname for the system or use a Fully Qualified Domain Name (FQDN).

11. Once you have specified the network, you can toggle the Ethernet button on top to ON to switch on the network. If you have a router that has a DHCP, it will allocate the IPs to the respective devices, and your IP will now be visible. If not, you can click on the Configure button to manually specify the settings for your network.

12. Once you have configured the Ethernet settings, click on Done, and you will be presented with the Installation screen. You will get one last chance to review your installation settings before the setup starts writing files to your disk. After reviewing, click on the Begin Installation option to start the installation.

13. The installation will now start writing files to your hard disk. Meanwhile, you will be prompted to create a new user for your system along with a password. Click on Root Password and supply a password that is strong and has at least eight characters with a combination of the alphabet and numbers. Click on Done

14. Next, you can create a new user other than root and provide the credentials for this user. We recommend that you make this new user a system administrator who will have privileges similar to the root user by using the sudo command. So check the box, which says, "Make this user administrator," and then click Done. Give the installation some time to complete.

15. Once the installation is complete, you will see a message confirming the same and that you can now reboot the system and get ready to use it

Voila! You can now unplug your installation media, which is the USB drive and restart your computer. You will be presented with the login screen for a minimal installation of Red Hat Enterprise Linux

7. You can either use the root user or the additional user that you created to login to the system.

This information will be helpful to understand the automated kickstart installation process better, which we will see in the section that follows.

Overview of Kickstart Installations

The kickstart feature of Red Hat Enterprise Linux allows a system administrator to automate the installation of Red Hat Enterprise Linux. The installer of Red Hat is known as Anaconda. Specific parameters need to be passed to anaconda so that it knows what to do during the installation process. These are as follows.

1. Network interface configurations

2. Disk partitions

3. Packages to be installed

The installation process is very interactive. The kickstart process uses a text file in which the above parameters are defined, which eliminates the need for interaction.

Note: The kickstart feature in Red Hat Linux is similar to the Jumpstart feature in Oracle Solaris, and an unattended installation in Microsoft Windows.

There is a list of commands in the kickstart configuration file that describes how the installation process is to be carried out on the target machine. Lines beginning with # are comments in the file and are ignored when the installation is ongoing. Then some sections start with the % character and end with the %end string.

The section under %packages specifies the software to be installed on the target system. Packages are defined individually by specifying just the name without any version numbers. A group of packages can be specified using a name or an ID and begin with the @ character. Environment groups, which are groups of package groups, are defined using the @^ character. They are immediately followed by the name or ID of the environment group. There are components for groups that are default, mandatory, or optional. Kickstart will usually install the default and mandatory components. There are group names and packages preceded by the - symbol. These are discarded from the kickstart installation unless they are dependencies of other packages or are mandatory.

There are two additional sections for scripts in the file, which are defined using %pre and %post. %post scripts are standard and are responsible for system configuration after the installation has concluded. The %pre script runs before the installation of packages and before the disk is partitioned.

The commands for configuration must occur first in the kickstart configuration file. The %packages, %pre, and %post do not necessarily need to be in a specific order after the configuration commands.

Commands for the Kickstart Configuration File

Installation Commands

URL: The location for the installation media is specified in this command.

URL -- ftp://installationmediaserver.com/pub/RHEL7/dvd."

Repo: This option specifies the package repository for the installation. It must point to a valid yum repository.

repo -- name="Custom Packages" ---
baseurl="ftp://repo.installtion.com/custom"

Text: Enforces an installation in text mode.

Vnc: If there is a graphical installation, it can be viewed remotely using VNC.

vnc --password=redhatlinux

Askmethod: This ensures that the CD-ROM is not automatically used as the source for packages when there are installation media in the CD-ROM drive.

Partitioning Commands

- Clearpart: You can clear the specified partitions before the installation begins.

  clearpart --all --drives=sda, sdc --initlabel

- Part: The name, format, and size for a partition are specified using this parameter.

  part /home --fstype=ext4 --label=myhome --size= 4096 -- maxsize=8192 --grow

- Ignoredisk: The disk specified for this parameter is ignored during the installation.

  ignoredisk --drives=sdb

- Bootloader: The disk for the bootloader installation is specified using this parameter.

  bootloader --location=mbr --boot-drive=sda

- Volgroup, logvol: Used to create logical volumes and LVM volume groups.

  part pv.01 --size=8192

volgroup myvg pc.01

logvol / --vgname=myvg --fstype=xfs --size=4096 -- name=volroot --grow

logvol var --vgname=myvg --fstype=xfs --size=4096 -- name=volvar --grow

- Zerombr: Disks that have unrecognized formatting are initialized.

Network Commands

- Network: The network-related information is configured for the target system, and all the network devices in the environment are activated.

Network --device=eth0 --bootproto=dhcp

- Firewall: The firewall configuration for the target system is defined using this parameter.

firewall --enabled --service=cups, ssh

Configuration Commands

- Lang: The language specified here will set the language to be used throughout the installation, and it will also be the default system language after installation.

lang en_US.UTF-8

- Keyboard: The type of keyboard is set for the system.

keyboard --vckeymap=us --xlayouts='us', 'us'

- Timezone: The time zone, NTP servers, and whether or not the hardware clock used UTC are defined using this parameter.

timezone --utc --ntpservers=exampletime.com
Europe/Amsterdam

- Auth: The authentication algorithms for the system are set up using this parameter.

  auth --useshadow --enablemd5 --passalgo=sha256

- Rootpw: The root password for the system is set up using this parameter.

  rootpw --plaintext redhatlinux

- Selinux: The state for SELinux is set up on the target system.

  selinux --enforcing

- Services: The state of the default services that run in the default run level is modified.

  services   --disable=network,   ip6tables,   iptables   --
  enabled=firewalld,   NetworkManager

- Group, user: A user or a local group is created on the system using this parameter.

  group --name=admins gid=10003

  User --name=john --gecos="John De" --groups=admins --
  password=newpassword --plaintext

Miscellaneous Commands

- Logging: The logging for anaconda during installation is defined using this parameter.

  logging --host=loghost.com --level=info

- Firstboot: Define if firstboot should be enabled or disabled when the system is booted.

  firstboot --disabled

- Reboot, halt, and poweroff: Specifies the action to be taken after installation concludes.

This is how a sample kickstart file for RHEL7 looks like:

Kickstart configuration for RHEL7

Additional repo to be used for installation

repo --name="Installation" --
baseurl=file:///run/installationmedia/repoitory/Packages

platform=AMD64, or x86

System authorization information

auth --enableshadow --passalgo=sha256

Clear the Master Boot Record

zerombr

Partition clearing information

clearpart --all --initlabel

Use text mode install

text

Firewall configuration

firewall --enabled

Run the Setup Agent on first boot

firstboot --enable

System keyboard

keyboard us

System language

lang en_US.UTF-8

Installation logging level

logging --level=info

Use NFS installation media

nfs --server=10.42.137.1 --dir=/home/repo/rhel7

Network Information

network --bootproto=static --hostname=deep-node3 --device=eth0 --
gateway=192.168.10.100 --ip=192.168.10.1 --
netmask=255.255.255.0 --noipv6 --nodns --onboot=on --activate

network --bootproto=static --device=eth1 --gateway=192.168.10.100
--ip=192.168.10.2 --netmask=255.255.255.0 --noipv6 --nodns --
onboot=on --activate

network --bootproto=static --device=eth2 --gateway=192.168.10.100
--ip=192.168.10.3 --netmask=255.255.255.0 --noipv6 --nodns --
onboot=on --activate

System bootloader configuration

bootloader --location=mbr --driveorder=sdb --append="rhgb novga
console=ttyS0,9600 console=tty0 crashkernel=showopts panic=1
numa=off noht"

Disk Partitioning

```
clearpart --all --initlabel

part /boot --size 512 --asprimary --fstype=ext4 --ondrive=sda

part pv.1 --size 1 --grow --fstype=ext4 --ondrive=sda

volgroup system --pesize=32768 pv.1

logvol / --fstype ext4 --vgname system --size=4096 --name=root

logvol /var --fstype ext4 --vgname system --size=4096 --name=var

logvol /tmp --fstype ext4 --vgname system --size=40960 --
name=tmp

logvol swap --vgname system --size=4096 --name=swap

logvol /var/log --fstype ext4 --vgname system --size=1 --grow --
name=varlog

# Root password

rootpw --redhatlinux

# SELinux configuration

selinux --enabled

# System timezone

timezone --UTC America/Los_Angeles

# Install OS instead of upgrade

install

# Switch off after installation

power off

# list of packages to be installed
```

```
%packages
@ Core
@ Base --nodefaults
bc
device-mapper-multipath
Ipmitool
 dos2unix
Ksh
 java
Rsync
 python-devel
Sos
 screen
Vim-enhanced
 syslinux
xinetd
#ExtraPackages
Perl-Switch
# packages deleted according to OS minimization
-firewalld
-iwl2000-firmware
```

-iwl5150-firmware

-iwl3160-firmware

packages added according to OS minimization

%end

%post --log=/var/log/kickstart_post.log

echo "Installation has Completed" > /tmp/installresult.out

date >> /tmp/installresult.out

%end

Deploying Virtual Systems Using Kickstart

In this section, we learn how to use the system-config-kickstart utility to make a new kickstart configuration. We will also learn how to modify an existing kickstart configuration file and use the ksvalidator tool to verify if the syntax in the kickstart configuration file is correct. We will learn how to publish a kickstart configuration file to the installer and also how to perform a kickstart network installation.

The process needs to be in an ordered format so that the installation of Red Hat Enterprise Linux is successful.

Kickstart installation is performed using the steps mentioned below.

1. The creation of the kickstart configuration file

2. Publishing the kickstart installation file to the installer

3. Booting Anaconda and referencing it to the kickstart configuration file

Kickstart Configuration File Creation

The kickstart configuration file can be created in two ways.

- By using a text editor

- By using the system-config-kickstart utility

When you use the system-config-kickstart utility, there will be multiple graphical dialog boxes that will popup, asking you to enter your choices. With these choices, a text file is created for the kickstart configuration as configured by the user in the graphical dialog boxes. Every dialog box that pops up will ask you to enter one or the other parameters required for the Red Hat Enterprise Linux installation. You can also use an existing configuration file for kickstart in the system-config-kickstart utility, and the dialog boxes will correspond to the values passed in the configuration file. The system-config-kickstart package provides the system-config-kickstart utility.

On the other hand, you'll rarely find someone creating a text configuration file for kickstart from scratch. If you already have a system on which Red Hat Enterprise Linux has been installed, you will find a file created by Anaconda at /root/anaconda-ks.cfg. This file contains the parameters that need to be passed in the kickstart configuration file and can be used as a template to automate future installations.

The following reasons show why some system admins prefer using a text file for kickstart over the system-config-kickstart utility.

- If there is no GUI which would mean that the system-config-kickstart utility would not be available

- If the disk partitioning scheme needs to be advanced. system-config-kickstart utility does not support RAID or LVM

- If you need to install individual software packages

- If you need to include advanced %pre and %post scripts

The ksvalidator utility helps check for any syntax errors in the kickstart configuration file. The utility checks if the options and keywords in the file are proper, but will not check the values passed for options, as those are custom values. It will also skip anything in the %pre and %post scripts section. For example, if the firewall -- disabled option has not been spelled correctly, one of the following errors would be generated.

[root@server] ksvalidator /home/kickstartfile.cfg

The following problem occurred on line 9 of the kickstart file:

Unknown command: firewall

The pykickstart RPM provides ksvalidator tool in Red Hat Enterprise Linux.

Publishing the Kickstart Installation File to the Installer

The Anaconda installer needs to be able to access the kickstart configuration file so that it can start the installation. There are several methods through which the anaconda installer can access the kickstart file, but the most common methods are through a network server, which can be a web server, an FTP server, or an NFS server. Another way to provide the kickstart configuration files is through a CD-ROM or a USB. To install Red Hat Linux, you will be using a boot media device such as a USB or a CD-ROM, and the kickstart configuration file can be embedded in the same media as well.

The kickstart configuration file could be saved on the local hard disk as well. This will help to rebuild a development server without wasting much time.

Booting Anaconda and Referencing it to the Kickstart Config File

It is important to tell the Anaconda installer about the kickstart configuration file's location if you are using the kickstart method. This can be achieved by passing the following argument in the installation kernel.

ks=LOCATION

A few of the sample locations are as follows.

- ks=http://server.dir/file

- ks=ftp://server/dir/file

- ks=hd:device:/dir/file

If you are trying to install Red Hat Enterprise Linux on a virtual machine using the kickstart method, the location for the kickstart file can be specified in the box available in URL options. This will be available in the Virtual Machine Manager or virt-manager utility.

CHAPTER 2

Grep with Regular Expressions

In the first book of this series, we learned about the grep command. This command is used to look for a string in the file. In this chapter, we will learn how to use grep with regular expressions, which make the grep tool even more powerful and helpful. We will learn how to use the grep command to write regular expressions to isolate content or to locate content in text files. This will be achieved by writing regular expressions to match text patterns.

Fundamentals of Regular Expressions

"Regular expressions" is a language for pattern matching used by many applications so that they can go through data and find the desired content. In addition to applications such as grep, vim, and less, which use regular expressions, it is also used on a vast scale by other programming languages such as Python, Perl, C, etc. for pattern-matching tasks.

Regular expressions exist as an independent language, and therefore, also have their own rules and syntax. In this section, we will learn about the syntax used for regular expressions and also go through some examples to understand regular expressions better.

A Simple Regular Expression

The simplest regular expression is an exact match. When the characters in the regular expression match the order and type of the data being searched, it will be an exact match.

Suppose there is a file with data, and the user needs to search for data, which will be an exact match of the string "cat."

cat

dog

dogma

concatenate

category

chilidog

educated

The exact match of the cat would be c, followed by a, followed by t. If we use the regular expression cat in the file mentioned above, the output will be as follows.

cat

concatenate

category

educated

Line Anchors

In the previous section, we used exact match regular expressions to search through a file with data in it. If you observed carefully, you would have noticed that for an exact match, it does not have a rule that the required string should be at the beginning of the line, in the middle, or at the end of a line. The line anchor helps you to look for a match based on the location of the match.

The following line anchors are available in Red Hat Enterprise Linux.

^: If you are looking for a match at the beginning of the line

$: If you are looking for a match at the end of the line

Let us consider the same file which we used earlier with the following data.

cat

dog

dogma

concatenate

category

chilidog

educated

You can use the ^cat regular expressions such that it would match only if it occurs at the beginning of the line. The output for this would be cat

category

If we used $dog regular expression, it would search for the word dog at the end of the line. The output for this would be

dog

chilidog

If you wanted to ensure that the pattern you specified was the only thing on a line in the file, you could use both ^ and $ around the pattern. For example, if you wanted to find cat exactly, you could use the regular expression as ^cat$, the output of this regular expression from the file above would only be

Cat

Wildcards and Multipliers

The character used for wildcards in regular expressions is a period(.) Say if you supplied a regular expression c.t, it will look for any data that starts with c, has one character in the middle, and ends with t. So the output of this regular expression can be cat, cut, cot, etc. and also something like c5t.

Another set of wildcards that are used in regular expressions are acceptable characters in a given position. For example, if you need to match data, which starts with c and ends with t, but want to leave out the odd data such as c5t, you can use the following wildcard, which will only search for the specific characters in the specified location. So if you specify the regular expression with a wildcard like c[aou]t, it will look for data which starts with c, ends with t, and the central character is a, o, or u. Therefore, the output of this will only be cat, cot, or cut.

Multipliers are used with wildcards very often. Multipliers take into consideration the previous character in a regular expression. A standard multiplier is *.A*, which, when used with a regular expression, modifies the previous character to mean zero to infinitely many of that character. If a regular expression of c.*t were specified, it would match ct, cot, coat, covert, etc. This means that the compiler can look for any string that starts with 'c' and end with 't' with zero to infinite characters in between them.

Another multiplier that can be used with a regular expression is the one that indicates exactly how many previous characters are desired in the pattern. For example, if we used the following multiplier in a regular expression c.\{2\}t, the output will contain all matching data that begins with c, ends with t, and has exactly two characters in between them.

Using Grep to Match the Text

In this section, we will learn how to use grep with the common options available for grep. We will learn how to use grep with piped commands to search files and data.

Using Grep

Grep is a command, which is a part of the Red Hat Enterprise Linux distribution, which combines with regular expressions to isolate matching data.

Grep Usage

The basic function of grep is to specify a regular expression and a file on which the regular expression needs to be matched.

[student@server~]$ grep 'cat$' /var/log/maillog

The grep command can be combined with other command using a pipe |

[root@server~]# ps aux | grep '^admin'

Options in Grep

Several options can be used with grep to adjust the regular expressions used with it.

Option	Function
-i	This will ensure that case sensitivity is not enforced. The matching function will run as case-insensitive
-v	This will display all the lines that DO NOT match the regular expression
-r	The regular expression match function will run recursively through directories and files
-A \<number>	This will display the \<number> of lines after a match was found for the regular expression
-B \<number>	This will display the \<number> of lines before a match was found for the regular expression
-e	This is used to supply multiple regular expressions and will be used with a logical OR operator

CHAPTER 3

· ·

Vim Text Editor

In this chapter, we will learn about Vim, which is a tool for creating and editing text files in the Red Hat Enterprise Linux distribution. We will learn about the three modes of vim. We will learn to edit and save text files in vim and use the shortcuts available in vim.

In this section, we will learn about the three main modes of vim.

Introduction to Vim

As a Linux system administrator, editing files will be one of the tasks you end up regularly doing. There are many text editors available for Linux systems. One of the older text editor, which was used widely, is vi. Vi stands for visual interface, as it was one of the first text editors that showed the document while it was being edited. Before vi, there were only line-based editors such as ed and ex. vim is an improved version of vi.

The version of vi, which comes prebuilt in Red Hat Enterprise Linux, is vim. vim stands for Vi improved as vim has many new features not available previously, but is still backward compatible. A few of the new features are the syntax, highlighting, spell-check, and completion modes.

Vim is highly extensible. It has support for scripts in multiple languages, various text completion modes, file type plugins, and many other options. It can adapt to any role. There are third party macros and extensions available for vim on the internet for any purpose, from editing a particular type of file, completion, and introspection for all available programming languages, to simple tasks such as to-do lists.

Is it Necessary to Learn Vim?

As a system administrator, you will have a preference for a text editor. Some people use nano, others use gedit, and some even use emacs. Even if you already have a choice for an editor, it still makes sense to learn the basics of vi or vim because, by default, vim and vim are installed on every Linux distribution.

Different Versions of Vim

The Red Hat Enterprise Linux supports three different versions of vim. There are use cases for every version, but all three versions can be used and run side by side. The following three variations are available.

- Vim-minimal: This package only contains vi and related commands. The minimal installation of Red Hat Enterprise Linux comes with this version of vim.

- Vim-enhanced: This package comes with vim, providing features such as spell check, syntax highlighting, and file type plugins.

- Vim-X11: This package comes with gvim, a version of vim, which has a graphical window instead of running on the terminal. The best feature of gvim is the menu bar, which is useful for new learners of vim who can't remember specific commands. Depending on the type of terminal and the configuration of the user, it is also possible to use a mouse inside a regular vim session.

Modes of Vim

Vim is not exactly a straightforward editor. The commands available in vim aim at efficiency and speed, and not exactly ease of remembrance. This is because vim has many modes. This means that the function of keys and commands change based on the vim mode that is currently active.

Vim has the following three modes.

Function	Mode
Command mode	In this mode, you can do file navigation, cut, copy and paste functions, and other simple commands. Commands like undo and redo can also be performed in this mode
Insert mode	Normal text editing can be performed in this mode. There is a variation of insert mode known as replace mode in which you can replace text instead of inserting it
Ex mode	Functions such as opening a file, saving it, or quitting vim can be performed in this mode. It also supports a few other complex functions. The output of programs can be inserted into the current file using this mode. Vim configurations can be done from this mode as well. Everything that one can perform in ex can be done in this mode of vim

Vim Workflow

In this section, we will learn how to open text files, move the cursor in vim, insert and replace text, save files, and look at help options.

Editor Basics

Irrespective of the editor being used, you should always be able to perform these three primary tasks.

1. Create a new file or open an existing one

2. Make changes to the file or add new text to a file

3. Save the changes and exit

Opening Files

Vim allows you to open files easily on the command line by specifying the filename as an argument. For example, if you wanted to open a file at /var/log/maillog where maillog is the file, you could use the following command.

[root@server~]# vim /var/log/maillog

Note: If the file specified as an argument does not exist, but the directory is valid, vim will create a new file with the filename specified and inform you that you are editing a new file.

Vim will open in the command mode by default. The bottom left corner of the screen gives information about the opened file such as filename, number of characters, number of lines, etc. It also displays information about the part of the file being shown, such as All for all, Top for the lines at the top, Bot for the last lines of the file, or a percentage which shows what part of the file you are at. The last line is called the ruler in vim terminology.

Editing Text

If you have already used vi or vim, you will know that keys do not work the way they should when you are in command mode. This is because command mode is not used to insert text but rather to perform functions based on the characters you type, such as copy and paste, or cursor movements.

You can switch to insert mode by using a set of commands that correspond to different functions. Let's go through them one by one.

The key and result for the same in as mentioned:

Key	Result
i	This will switch you to the insert mode, and you can start typing before the current position of the cursor
a	This will switch you to insert mode as well but will start typing after the current position of the cursor
I	Will move the cursor to the beginning of the current line and switch you to insert mode
A	Will move the cursor to the end of the current line and switch you to insert mode
R	Will switch you replace mode, starting at the character where the cursor currently is. You cannot insert additional characters in the replace mode, but every character you type replaces the current character in the given document.
o	A new line is opened below the current line, and you then switch to insert mode

O	A new line is opened above the current line, and you then switch to insert mode

You will know that you are in insert mode or replace mode by the indicator below which shows --INSERT-- or --REPLACE--

You can use the Esc key on the keyboard to return to command mode.

The version of vi or vim that comes with Red Hat Enterprise Linux is preconfigured to identify normal movements of the cursor, and even PgUp and End while you are in both command mode and insert mode. This is not the default settings for all variations of vi but is specific to Red Hat Enterprise Linux. Older versions of vi did not recognize these commands, and you could only move the cursor while in command mode using keyboard keys h, j, k, l.

The following table lists down some common keys that can be used to move the cursor while you are in command mode.

Key	Result
h	The cursor is moved to the left by one position
j	The cursor is moved down by one line
k	The cursor is moved up by one line
l	The cursor is moved to the right by one position
^	The cursor is moved to the start of the current line
$	The cursor is moved to the end of the current line

gg	The cursor is moved to the first line of the document
G	The cursor is moved to the last line of the document

Note: Pressing the Esc key on the keyboard will always cancel the current command or return you to the command mode of vim. A good practice is to press the Esc key twice or more to make sure that you have returned to the command mode.

Saving Files

The ex mode is used to save files in vim. To enter the ex mode, you need to press the colon (:) key on the keyboard while you are in the command mode. So if you are in the insert mode, first press the Esc key to switch to command mode and then press the colon to enter the ex mode. When you switch to the ex mode, you will see the ':' symbol on the ruler where you can proceed with typing a command. Once you are done typing a command, press enter to complete the command.

The following table gives a list of commands which will help you save your changes and quit vim in the ex mode.

Command	Result
:wq	Save the current file and quit vim
:x	Save the current file if there are no unsaved changes, and then quit vim
:w	Save the current file and stay in the editor. Does not quit vim

:w <filename>	Use a different filename to save the current file
:q	Quit the current file ONLY if there are no unsaved changes
:q!	Ignore any unsaved changes and quit the current file

In the table above, w stands for write, implying saving changes, q stands for quit, and ! indicates an action is to be forced.

Getting Help in Vim

There is extensive online help for vim, which is available through the editor itself. You can switch to command mode and type ':help,' and the help screen will be launched with the help needed to navigate through the help document. You can find help for a specific subject or topic by typing ':help subject' from the command mode.

The help screen will open in a new split window. You can close the help screen by typing :q. To get help with split windows, you can type :help windows.

A semi-interactive tutor is also available. While in the command mode, you can type the command vimtutor. This will launch a guided tour of vim, and a new user can learn the basics almost within an hour.

Editing with Vim

In this section, we will learn shortcuts for movement through vim while editing, copy and paste, use search and replace, and use the undo and redo options.

Movement in Vim

Most editors have navigation support with the limitation that you can move through only a single character or a single line. These single movement options are available in the command mode of vim as well. Additionally, there are some advanced commands in vim, which will help you navigate through a document more efficiently. These command shortcuts in vim will help you move through a document per word, sentence, or even a paragraph. However, do note that these movements for the cursor will only work in the command mode and not in the insert mode of vim.

Key	Function
w	The cursor is moved to the start of the next word
b	The cursor is moved to the start of the previous word
(	The cursor is moved to the start of the current sentence or the previous sentence
)	The cursor is moved to the start of the next sentence
{	The cursor is moved to the start of the current paragraph or the precious paragraph
}	The cursor is moved to the start of the next paragraph

You can use a number as a prefix to the commands mentioned above, as well. For example, 6w will move the cursor after the next six words, or 13(will move the cursor to the start of the line after 13 lines. This is known as count in the vim terminology.

Text Replacement

The change command in vim allows users to replace one word or more words of text. To execute the change command, you can press the c key on the keyboard and follow it with cursor movement. For example, cw will move the cursor from the current position to the end of the current word you are at. The text that you want to delete is replaced as vim switches to the insert mode.

Editing can be performed even more efficiently by using some shortcuts as follows.

- If you press the c key twice, cc, the replacement function will be performed per line. This will replace the entire line or the number of lines when prefixed with the number of lines. This same method applies to other functions as well, such as deleting a line or several lines.

- You can also prefix the movement commands with i or a to select a particular version of the movement. For example, using ciw will replace the entire current word, and not just from the current cursor position. You can also use c$, which will replace everything till the end of the line. This method again can be used for other actions such as deletion.

- You can use r to replace a single character under the cursor.

- If you want to change the case of the character under the cursor, you can use ~.

Text Deletion

The deletion of text works similar to the replacement of text. The d command is used to delete text in vim, and the same movements that apply to text replacement apply to text deletion as well. This includes the use of D to remove the text from the cursor's current position till the end of that line.

You can use x to delete the single character, which is under the cursor.

Copy and Paste

The copy and paste terminologies in vim are a bit different than what most users are used to. The operation for copy is known as yank, and the paste operation is known as put. The keyboard commands assigned for these operations are a reflection of this. Yank is represented by y, followed by the movement and put is represented by p or P.

The same schemas used for delete or replace are used by yank as well. Again, a number can be prefixed to repeat the operation a particular number of times. For example, 6aw will copy the current work along with the next six words. Using yy will copy the entire line.

The p and P commands are used for putting or pasting. The lower case p pastes the content after the cursor or below the current line while the upper case P pastes the content before the current position of the cursor, or above the current line. Like all the other commands, a number can be prefixed with the put command to perform multiple line puts.

Multiple Registers in Vim

In vim, instead of just one clipboard to store copied content, there are 26 named registers. Vim also has a few special registers, as well. Content can be copied and pasted more efficiently due to the presence of these registers, as users do not need to worry about the loss of data or to move the cursor too much. You can specify the register that you want to use. If it is not specified, vim makes use of the unnamed register. The normal registers are named from a to z. You can use these in your code by specifying "registername" between the count for the command and the actual command to be used. For example, if you want to copy the current line and the next three lines into the register t, you can use the command 3"tyy

If you wish to paste the content stored on a particular register, for example, register s, you can put the registername before the put command like sp.

Storing something in a named register automatically adds it to the unnamed register as well.

You can use a register with the delete and replace operations as well. Again, when there is no register specified, the unnamed default register is taken into consideration. If you use an uppercase version of the register, the text being yanked or cut gets appended to that particular register and does not overwrite it.

Special Registers

Special registers are numbered from 0 to 9. 0 stores a copy of the most recently copied text, and the value 1 stores a copy of the most recently deleted text.

Content in the named registers is retained across sessions. However, the content of the special registers is not retained between sessions.

Visual Mode in Vim

Vim also supports a visual mode so that you do not have to continually worry about counting the number of characters, lines, words, or sentences. The visual mode is indicated by --VISUAL-- in the vim ruler. You can use the visual mode to select text by just moving the cursor around. You do not need to move the cursor in the visual mode to use commands like replace, yank, or delete. It will automatically apply to the text that has been selected.

There are three flavors of visual mode.

1. The character-based visual mode which starts with v

2. The line-based visual mode which starts with V

3. The block-based visual mode which starts with Ctrl+V

While using the graphical mode of vim, you can also use the mouse to select text.

Searching in Vim

There are two ways to start a search in a given document.

1. If you press the / key, the search will search after the cursor position in the current document

2. If you press the ? key, the search will scan through the document behind the current position of the cursor

You can use a regular expression in the search mode to search the document and find a match. The next and the previous match can be searched using the n and N keys, respectively.

Useful shortcut: If you have a word under the cursor and want to search for the same word in the document, you can use the * key to search its very next occurrence in the document.

Search and Replace in Vim

The ex mode is used to implement search and replace in vim. The regular expressions such as ranges, patterns, strings, and flags can be used to implement search and replace.

The range can be a particular line number or a range of line numbers, or even a search term to match all the lines in the current document.

The search and replace functions usually applies only to the current line or the current visual selection in the visual mode.

Example of search and replace:

Consider a document that has the word cat at multiple locations, and you wish to replace it with the word dog, irrespective of its case, and given that it is an independent word and not a part of some string such as catalog. In this scenario, you could use the following command.

:%s/\<cat\>/dog/gi

Undo and Redo

There are undo and redo mechanisms supported by vim as well to cover human errors. An undo action can be performed in the command mode by pressing u. If you end up undoing too many things, you can use the Ctrl+r command to redo an action.

Bonus: If you press the period '.' key in the command mode, it will undo the previous action but only on the current line.

CHAPTER 4

* · + ——————— · + · · + · ——————— + · ·

Scheduling Tasks in Linux

In this chapter, we will learn how to schedule tasks in Linux to be automatically executed in the future. This will be achieved by scheduling one-time tasks using at and using cron to schedule recurring tasks. We will also look at how to schedule recurring jobs and manage temporary files.

Scheduling One-Time Tasks Using At

After completing this section, you will be proficient in scheduling one time tasks in Linux using at.

Scheduling Future Tasks

From time to time, a Linux system admin or even a regular use would want to define tasks to execute at a specific time in the future. An example of this would be a regular employee who wants to schedule an email to be sent to their manager or a client or a Linux system admin who wants to make some configurations in the system's firewall so that the firewall resets, say, every ten minutes. These commands, which are executed in a scheduled manner, are known as jobs or tasks.

Using 'at' to Schedule One-Time Tasks

One of the options available to a system admin in Red Hat Enterprise Linux is to schedule one-off tasks. This is not an independent tool but is part of a system daemon called atd, which provides a few command-line tools so that you can interact with the daemon. The atd daemon is available and activated by default in a Red Hat Enterprise Linux distribution. The atd daemon is available via the 'at' package.

The command-line tool 'at' can be used by the root user and other users to queue up tasks for the atd daemon. There are 26 queues available in the atd daemon from a to z. The priority of the jobs in this queue depends on the order in which they are placed between a to z, where a has the highest priority, and z has the least priority.

Scheduling Jobs

You can use the command at <TIMESPEC> to schedule a new job. The command will be picked up by at, and it will execute these commands from stdin. If the commands are of bigger length, or if you do not want to have errors in case sensitivity, it is advisable to input the commands from a script file over typing all the commands manually from the command line.

at now +5min < scriptfile

If you are typing out commands manually on the command line, you can use the Ctrl+D key to complete your command.

The <TIMESPEC> input works for various formats allowing a user to use a free-form way to specify the exact time for the job or task to be executed. You could specify it as 02.00 pm, 15:45, or even something like teatime. This can be optionally followed by a date or the number of days for which you want the task to run.

Inspecting and Managing Jobs

If you need an overview of the jobs that are still pending to be executed, you can use the command atq or its alias at -1.

The output of this command is as follows.

[user@server~]$ atq

28 Mon Jan 3 05:12:00 2017 a user

The above output has four columns for every job scheduled to execute in the future.

- The first column shows the job number, 28

- The second column shows the date and time scheduled for the job to execute. Mon Jan 3 05:12:00

- The third column shows the queue for the job, a

- The last column shows the user who created and owns the job

A typical user will be able to see only the jobs that have been created by them. The root user, however, has access to see jobs created by all users in the system.

To see the actual command that will be executed when the job runs, you can use the command at -c <JOBNUMBER>. The output will show the environment in which the job was set up, which reflects the environment of the user who created the job. This will be followed by the actual command listed in the job.

Removing Jobs

If you wish to remove a job that you created, as you feel it is no longer needed, you could use the command atrm <JOBNUMBER>.

Scheduling Recurring Jobs using Cron

An Overview of Cron

It is possible to set up recurring jobs using at as well in theory. This could be done by executing a job which, after it concludes, initiates another job. However, this is poor if practiced in reality. Therefore, the Red Hat Enterprise Linux system comes with the crond daemon, which is enabled and activated by default for scheduling recurring jobs or tasks. There are user-based configuration files, one per user, as well as system-wide configuration files for crond. These configuration files give fine-tuning access to both users and system administrators to define when precisely their recurring tasks should be executed. The crond daemon is installed as a part of the cronie package.

If the output of a cron job does not produce any output on stdout or stderror, it is by default emailed to the owner of the cron job by using the mail server on the system, unless overridden exclusively. This may also need more configuration depending on the environment of the system.

Scheduling Cron Jobs

The crontab command can be used by normal users to create and manage cron jobs. There are four ways in which this command can be used.

Command	Result
crontab -l	All the jobs for the current user are listed
crontab -r	All the jobs for the current users are removed
crontab -e	To edit jobs that have been already created by the user

crontab <filename>	All the jobs for the current user are removed and are then replaced by the jobs listed in the filename. stdin will be used if the user does not specify a filename

The root user can use the command -u <username>to manage jobs created by another user. System jobs need not use the crontab command. We will discuss this later.

Format for a Job

When you use the crontab -e command to edit jobs, an editor is launched by default. You can define one job per line in the file that opens. You can leave the lines empty in the file. You can use the hash # symbol to change the lines in the code that you do not want to execute to comments. You can define environment variables as well using the format NAME=value. The SHELL and MAILTO are the most common environment variables declared in a crontab. The SHELL variable tells the crontab which shell is used to execute the job, and the MAILTO variable tells crontab which email address to send the output to.

Note: Email functionality for the crontab requires a mail server to be configured on the system.

There are a total of six fields specified in individual jobs that indicated what should be executed and when it should be executed. When the first five fields match the current data and time, the command given in the last field is executed.

- Minutes
- Hours
- Day of the month
- Month
- Day of the week
- Command

Note: If the day of the month and day of the week field are not a wildcard *, the command will be executed when either of the two fields matches the current day. The application of this is that a command can be run on the 14th of every month and every Thursday.

The Syntax for the Fields

The first five fields all share the same syntax as follows.

4. * always indicated or don't care

5. A number which indicates the number of minutes, hours, date, or a weekday. For days of the week, 0 represents Sunday, 1 for Monday, and so on. But seven also represents a Sunday

6. x-y for a range where everything between x and y is included

7. x, y for lists. You can specify ranges as a part of the list such as 5, 6-10, 11

8. */x indicates an interval. For example, */7 will ensure that a job runs every seven minutes.

In addition to this, months and days of the week can also be specified using three-letter abbreviations in English.

The last field will have the command that needs to be executed. By default, the /bin/sh shell will execute the command, unless another SHELL environment variable has been exclusively declared. I there is a percentage % sign in the command, everything after the percentage is treated as a new line, and it will also be fed as input to the command at sdtin.

Cron Job Examples

1. 0 9 2 2* /usr/local/yearly_backup

   This will run the backup script at /usr/local/yearly_backup on February 2 every year at sharp 9 am

2. */7 9-16 * Jun 6 echo "Hello"

   An email containing the word Hello will be sent to the owner of the cron job at an interval of seven minutes between 9 am and 4 pm every Friday in June.

Scheduling Cron Jobs for the System

In this section, we will discuss how you can set up recurring jobs for the system.

System cron jobs

Apart from cron jobs set by a user, there are also cron jobs that can be set for the system.

Unlike user cron jobs, system cron jobs are not declared using the crontab command. They are instead declared using a few configuration files. The primary difference for jobs declared in crontab and configuration file is an extra field that lies between the day of the week and the command field. This extra field defines the user under whom the command should be run.

If you open the file at /etc/crontab, you will find a diagram for the syntax of system cron jobs.

There are two locations on the Red Hat Enterprise Linux system where you can define the system cron jobs.

3. /etc/crontab

4. /etc/cron.d/*

Packages that install cron jobs should be placed in a file under /etc/crond./ but as a Linux system admin, you could also use this location to store a file that has a group of related jobs in it or to push jobs using a configuration management system.

The Red Hat Enterprise Linux system also has a set of predefined jobs that will run automatically every hour, day, week, or month. These jobs execute any script that is placed in the following locations.

- /etc/cron.hourly/

- /etc/cron.daily/

- /etc/cron.weekly/

- /etc/cron.monthly/

Note: The files in these locations are scripts or jobs that you want to execute and do not contain and configuration files for cron. It is also important to make all scripts placed in the above locations executable using the chmod +x command.

The scripts in /etc/cron.hourly/ are executed with the help of the run-parts command, from another job which is declared at /etc/cron.d/0hourly. The run-parts command is also used to execute the daily, weekly, and monthly scripts, but the configuration for these is picked from a different location: /etc/anacrontab

Previously, /etc/anacrontab was managed by a separate daemon known as anacron, but in Red Hat Enterprise Linux 7, it is managed by the regular crond daemon. This file ensures that all the critical jobs execute without any failure, such as the system being turned off or in hibernation mode at the time the job was supposed to be executed.

The syntax of /etc/anacrontab differs from the regular configuration files for cron. There are four fields define per line.

- Period in day: Once per how many days the job should be executed.

- Delay in minutes: The amount of time the cron daemon will wait before triggering the job.

- Job Identifier: This field shows the name of the file in /var/spool/anacron/ which is used to check if the job was executed. When a job from /etc/anacrontab is executed by cron, the timestamp for that job will be logged in the file at /var/spool/anacron/. The same timestamp also lets you know the last time a particular job was executed.

- Command: The command to be executed is placed in this field.

In addition to this, you can also declare environment variables in the /etc/anacrontab file using the syntax NAME=value. One interesting environment variable is START_HOURS_RANGE. The jobs will not start before this time matches the current time.

Managing Temporary Files

In this section, we will learn about the systemd-tmpfiles utility and how it can be used to manage temporary files.

Temporary Files Management using systemd-tmpfiles

You would be well aware that there are a lot of temporary files and directories created in every modern system. There are specific visible directories for temporary files such as /tmp, which are used and more so abused by system users. Still, at the same time, there are temporary files and directories which are application-specific, daemon specific, or user-specific stored under /run. The directories mentioned in the latter part are volatile, meaning that they exist only in memory. This implies that if the system goes through a reboot or a power failure, the content of these volatile directories will be erased and lost.

These files are important as they keep the system running cleanly, given that individual scripts and daemons may rely on these files for their functioning. It is also important that old and unused temporary files be deleted from time to time so that they do not merely occupy space or end up giving erroneous information.

Previously, system admin used SystemV init-scripts and RPM packages to create these scripts. Similarly, a tool called tmpwatch was used to delete unused temporary files from the system.

This has changed in Red Hat Enterprise Linux 7. The systemd daemon in Red Hat Enterprise Linux 7 provides a more structured method to manage temporary files and directories using systemd-tmpfiles.

When a system is initiated using systemd, systemd-tmpfiles setup is one of the first services that is launched. The service triggers the command systemd-tmpfiles --create-- remove. The command then reads from certain configuration files. If it finds files and directories in these configuration files marked for deletion, it will remove those files. Similarly, any files and directories marked for creation will be created while maintaining the necessary ownerships and permissions.

Regular Cleaning

To ensure that stale data, like the data from web servers, do not pile up on systems, there must be a timer in place which calls the systemd-tmpfiles --clean command regularly.

The units for the systemd timer are a part of a special systemd service. They have a [Timer] block, which defines how often the service should be started.

The configuration for the systemd timer is stored in systemd-tmpfiles-clean.timer in Red Hat Enterprise Linux. It looks like this.

[Timer]

OnBootSec=10min

OnUnitActiveSec=1d

This means that the service systemd-tmpfiles-clean.timer will run 10 minutes after systemd is initiated and after that, once every 24 hours.

systemd-tmpfiles configuration files

The syntax of the configuration files for systemd-tmpfiles consists of 7 columns.

- Type

- Path

- Mode

- UID

- GID

- Age

- Argument

Type indicates the action to be taken by systemd-tmpfiles such as d, which creates a directory if the directory does not exist, or Z, which restores file permissions and ownerships, and SELinux context in a recursive fashion.

Let us go through a few examples.

d /run/systemd/seats 0755 root root -

This command will create the directory /run/systemd/seats while creating other files and directories if it already does not exist. The owner of the new directory will be root, and the group assigned to it will also be root. The permissions set for the directory will be 0755. The directory is excluded from getting purged automatically.

D /home/admin/ 0700 admin admin 1d

This command will create the directory /home/admin if it does not exist. If it does exist, all its content will be emptied. When the systemd-tmpfiles --clean command runs, all the files that have not been accessed, modified or change for more than one day will be removed.

L /run/fstablink - root root - /etc/fstab

A symbolic link called /run/fstablink will be created, which will point to /etc/fstab. This line will never be purged automatically.

CHAPTER 5

Linux Process Priority Management

In this chapter, we will learn about Linux process priorities and how to change them. We will also learn about something known as nice levels and further set nice levels on new and existing processes.

Process Priority and Nice Concepts

After completing this section, you will be able to define nice levels and the effect they have.

Process Scheduling and Multitasking in Linux

The range of modern computers starts with the following:

- Single CPU or low-end processors which can perform only one individual instruction at a given point in time

- Multiple CPU or high-end processors come with multiple processors and cores which can perform hundreds of instructions parallelly.

Despite this vast difference, all these systems have one thing in common: The number of processes that need running always exceeds the number of cores available.

The only way for any Linux operating system or any other operating system to be able to run more processes than the number of cores available is by using a method known as time-slicing. Using this method, the time scheduler on an operating system can switch between multiple processes rapidly. This makes a user believe that multiple processes are running at the same time.

On a Linux based operating system, the kernel has a process scheduler that is responsible for this switching activity.

Relative Priorities

There will be important processes and those that are not. Thus, the scheduler can be instructed to use various scheduling policies for the various ongoing processes. SCHED_OTHER, which is also known as SCHED_NORMAL, is the scheduling policy used by the Linux process scheduler for most processes on a regular system. This being said, there are other policies available as well, which can be applied to processes as per your requirement.

The processes on a Linux system are not created equally. Therefore, processes with the SCHED_NORMAL policy can be assigned relative priority. This priority assigned to a process is called its nice value, and there are 40 levels of niceness a process can have.

The range of niceness level is from -20 to 19. A process will inherit a nice level from its parent process by default, and it is usually 0. If the nice level i high, it implies a lower priority. This would mean that this process will give up its CPU resources without any hesitation for other processes. If the nice level is low, it indicates a higher priority. This would mean that this process will not release its CPU resources easily. If there is no demand for CPU resources, perhaps during a time when the number of processes is less than the number of cores available, processes with a higher nice level will also use all the CPU resources available to them. But when the number of processes exceeds the number of CPU cores available, the

54

system will give less CPU time to processes with a high nice level as compared to processes with a low nice level.

Permissions and Nice Levels

Setting a lower nice level on a CPU resource-hungry process can result in a negative experience for other processes. Therefore, the root user who has a capability called CAP_SYS_NICE can set nice levels to negative and lower the nice levels of existing processes. Regular users with limited privileges can only set positive nice levels. Also, regular users can only raise the nice level on their processes but cannot change it back to lower values again.

There are many other methods to play with process priorities and the resources used by them than just nice levels. There are control groups known as cgroups, alternate scheduler policies and settings, and other methods. Nice levels are preferred because they are very easy to use, both by system admins and regular users.

Influencing Process Priorities by using Nice and Renice

In this section, we will launch processes by setting the nice level as NA for them. We will then modify their nice levels and report the nice levels for the processes.

Reporting on Nice Levels

There are various methods to view the nice levels in existing processes. There are process-monitoring tools such as the gnome-system-monitor, which show the nice level of a process by default, and if not, can be configured to show the nice levels.

Using the Top Command to Display Nice Levels

You can view running processes and manage them by using the top command. The default output of the top command will show two columns that are associated with the nice level. NI shows the actual nice level, while PR shows the nice level as mapped to a larger priority where a nice level of -20 corresponds to a priority of 0, and a nice level of 19 corresponds to a priority of 39.

Using the ps command to Display Nice Levels

Another command that can be used to display nice levels is ps. However, its default output will not show the nice levels of a process. Therefore a user will need to alter the output from ps in a way that the column for nice value is displayed. The column header itself is called nice. You can provide the nice parameter with the ps command so that the nice value is displayed in the output.

[user@server~]$ ps axo nice

Launching Processes with a Different Nice Value

As we have already discussed, a process usually inherits its nice value from its parent process when it is initially launched. This means that when we launch a process from the command line, it will inherit the nice value of the shell process from where it was launched. In most cases, the new process inherits a nice value of 0.

The nice tool is available to launch a process with a custom nice value, and it is available to both regular users and system admins. If you do not provide any options and run the command nice <COMMAND>, it will be assigned a nice value of 10. If you want to assign a custom nice level to the process, you can use the -n <NICELEVEL> parameter with the nice command. For example, if you want to start the command dogecoinminer with a nice level of 12 and push it to the background immediately, you need to use the following command.

[user@desktop~]$ nice -n 12 dogecoinminer &

Note: Regular users can only set a positive nice value between 0 to 19. The root user gets to set negative nice values as well between -20 to -1.

Changing the Nice Level of an Ongoing Process

The renice command is used to change the nice level on an existing process. The renice command has the following syntax.

Renice -n <NICELEVEL> <PID>...

For example, if you wish to change the nice level of the process hello@world to -7, you can use the following command as a system admin.

[root@desktop~]# renice -n -7 $(pgrep hello@world)

Note: You can specify more than one PID in a single command to change the nice levels of multiple processes.

Alternatively, you can also use the top command to change the nice level on a process. While the output of the top process is active, press r, followed by a process PID and the new nice level to change the nice level of that process.

CHAPTER 6

———•·•——————•·•—◆·•—•————————•·•—

Access Control Lists

In this chapter, our goal is to learn how to manage file security by using the POSIX access control lists known as ACLs. We will understand how to describe and manage POSIX access control lists.

POSIX Access Control Lists ACLs

In this section, we will learn about the access control lists and options for file system mounting. We will also learn how to view and interpret access control lists using commands like ls and getfacl. We will also discuss the access control lists mask and the permission precedence for access control lists.

The Concept of Access Control Lists

We have learned about Linux permissions in the previous book. Although permissions are useful in most situations, they have their limitations. The permissions for a file or a director are limited to the owner of the file, a group, or everyone else. It may not always be possible that the process will be a part of a file's group, and it will be a more serious issue to grant permission to everyone.

When you use access control lists, you can fine-tune the permissions to a file. Users or groups with names and users with a UID or groups with a GUID can be given permissions. Also, these permissions act over and above the standard permissions of the owner, group, or other file permissions.

The owner of the file has the right to set permissions for individual files or directories. Also, new files and directories created under existing ones can automatically inherit the ACLs set on the parent directory. Similar to the regular file access rules, at least the parent directory must have the permission of the other set to execute so that other users and groups have access.

Option for File System Mounting

It is necessary to mount the file system while keeping ACL support enabled. There is a built-in ACL for the XFS file system. Also, ext4 file systems created using Red Hat Enterprise Linux as the acl option, again enabled by default. However, ext4 systems from the previous versions of Red Hat Enterprise Linux need the acl option included with a mount request, or to be set on the superblock.

Viewing and Interpreting ACLs in Linux

When you use the ls -l command, you can only see a limited volume of information of the ACL in the output.

[user@desktop~]$ ls -l roster.txt

-rwxrw----+   1   user   controller   130   Mar 19 23:57 roster.txt

When you see a + symbol at the end of the permissions, you will know that there are additional access control lists settings on the file. You can interpret the user, group and other "rwx" flags as:

- user: The ACL settings are the same as the standard user file settings; rwx

- group: The group owner settings are not shown, but the current ACL mask settings are shown; rw

- Shows the ACL settings for others, which are the same as the stand user permissions for others; no access

Viewing ACLs of a File

The get the ACL settings set on a file, use the getfacl file command:

[user@desktop~]$ getfacl roster.txt

#file: roster.txt

#owner: user

#group: controller

user: rwx

user: james: ---

group:: rwx

group: sodor: r—

mask:: rw-

other:: ---

Let's take a look at each section of the example above.

The first three lines identify the name of the file and tell us who is the owner and group owner. If there are additional files for the flag, such as setgid or setuid, there will be a fourth line indicating which flag is set.

Then there are user entries with their permissions. There are group entries with their respective permissions. There are mask entries, and there are other entries.

You can get the FACL on a directory by using the getfacl /directory command.

[user@desktop~]$ getfacl .

#file: roster.txt

#owner: user

#group: controller

#flags: -s-

user: rwx

user: james: ---

 group:: rwx

 group: sodor: r—

 mask:: rwx

 other:: ---

default: other::---

default: group::rwx

The first three lines identify the name of the file and tell us who is the owner and group owner. If there are additional files for the flag, such as setgid or setuid, there will be a fourth line indicating which flag is set.

There are standard ACL entries.

user: rwx

user: james: ---

group:: rwx

group: sodor: r—

mask:: rw-

other:: ---

The ACL permissions seen here for the directory are the same as we saw on a file in the previous example. But these ACLs apply to the directories. The key difference is that all these entries are given additional execute permission. This is done so that they can perform a directory search function.

Then there are default entries, default group entries, default ACL mask entry, and default other entry.

The ACL Mask

The ACL mask determines the maximum number of permissions that can be given to named users, group owner, and named groups. The permissions of the other user or the file owner are not restricted. There will be an ACL mask on all files and directories using the ACL security feature.

You can view the mask using the getfacl command and even set a mask using the setfacl command. If you do not specify it exclusively, it will be calculated automatically, but it can also inherit the ACL mask from a parent directory mask setting. However, whenever an ACL is added, modified, or deleted, the mask is always recalculated.

ACL Permission Precedence

When determining whether a running process can access a file, ACLs and file permissions are applied as follows.

- The user ACL permissions apply if the process is running as the same user who owns the file.

- If the process is running as a user who is listed in the named user ACL entry, the named user ACL permissions apply.

- If the process is running as a group that matched the file's group owner, or as a group with an explicitly named group ACL entry, then the ACL permissions that match are applied.

- Otherwise, the ACL permissions of others get applied.

File Security using ACLs

In this section, we will be changing the regular ACL permissions of a file using setfacl. We will also learn how to control default ACL file permissions for new directories and files.

Modifying ACL File Permissions

Standard ACLs on files and directories can be added, modified, or removed using setfacl.

The normal file system representation of permissions is used by ACLs, as well.

- r for reading permission

- w for write permission

- x for execute permission

- A dash - indicates that there is no permission.

When you are using ACLs recursively to set permissions, you can use an uppercase X to instruct that the execute permission is to be set only for directories and not files. This behavior is the same as the chomod command.

Adding or Modifying an ACL

When you are setting an ACL on a file for the first time, and you do not mention the standard user, group, or other permissions, it will automatically inherit the default permissions of the file. The editor will also calculate a new mask value and assign it to the file as well.

You can use the following command to add or modify a user ACL or a named user ACL:

[user@desktop~]$ setfacl -m u:name:rX file

The name will be a username or a UID value. If it is blank, it will be applied to the file owner.

In this example, only read-only permissions are granted, and it already set, execute permissions as well.

The permissions of the ACL file owner and standard file owner are the same. Using setfacl on the file owner permissions is the same as using chmod on the file owner permissions. Chmod does not affect named users.

Recursive ACL Modifications

When you are applying an ACL to a directory, it will be common that you want to apply the ACL recursively to the files and directory structure. The -R option can be used to achieve this. A capital X is used while setting ACL recursively to ensure that files that already have the execute permission, retain it, and all directories are given the execute permission so that the search function works. It is also a good practice to use the capital X while setting ACL permissions non recursively, as it will prevent the error on a system admin's part to assign the execute permission to an unwanted file.

[user@desktop~]$ setfacl -R -m u:name:rX directory

This would add the user name to the directory and all existing files and subdirectories granting read-only and optional execute permissions.

Deleting ACL Entries

The syntax to delete ACL entries follows the same format as the modify option, except the ":perms" should not be specified

[user@desktop~]$ setfacl -x u:name, g:name directory

The named user and the named group is removed from the list of file ACLs or directory ACLs. All other existing ACLs will remain active.

Controlling ACL file Permissions

A directory can have a default ACL set on it, which will be inherited by all new files and subdirectories. Each of the standard ACL settings, including a default mask can have default ACL permissions set for them.

Default ACLs do not have access control for the directory as they only support ACL inheritance. This is why a directory still requires standard ACLs.

Let us look at an example:

[user@desktop~]$ setfacl -m d:u:name:rx directory

This command adds a default named user, d:u:name with read-only, and execute permissions on subdirectories.

CHAPTER 7

———•—+—•———————•—+—•—+—•————————+—•———

SELinux Security

The goal of this chapter is to manage the behavior of Security-Enhanced Linux (SELinux) in a system such that it can be secured against a possible compromise of the network service. We will understand the basic permissions in SELinux. We will use the setenforce to change the permissions of SELinux. We will change the context of a file using semanage and restorecon. We will set booleans for SELinux using setbool. We will also learn to examine logs to troubleshoot violations in SELinux using sealert.

Enabling and Monitoring SELinux

The objectives of this section are as follows.

- Understand the basics of permissions in SELinux and context transitions

- View the current mode of SELinux

- Interpret the SELinux context of a file properly

- Interpret the SELinux context of a process properly

- Identify the current boolean settings for SELinux

Basic Security Concepts in SELinux

Security-Enhanced Linux is an additional layer of security in Linux. SELinux helps to protect user data from system services that may have been compromised. The standard permissions security model of user/group/other are known to every system admin. This is a user and group-based model called discretionary access control. However, SELinux offers an additional object-based layer of security that used more sophisticated rules known as mandatory access control.

It is crucial to open firewall ports if access to the server has to be allowed remotely. However, this can damage the security, and hackers can find their way into the system. They can then compromise the processes of the webserver, get permissions: both of the apache user and the apache group. The apache user and group have read access to the document root, /var/ww/html, and write access to /tmp, /var/tmp/ and any other word-writable files or directories.

SELinux set security rules related to which process can access which files, ports, and directories. There is a special security label on every file, directory, process, and port known as the SELinux context. The SELinux policy uses the context to determine whether a process has access to a file, a directory, or a port. The SELinux policy does not allow any access by default unless defined otherwise explicitly. If there is no rule for allow, no access is given.

There are various contexts associated with SELinux labels such as user, type, role, and sensitivity. The type context is one on which all SELinux rules are based on in Red Hat Enterprise Linux. The names in type context usually end in _t. The type context for the webserver is httpd_t. The type context for regular files and directories is httpd_sys_content_t and is found in /var/www/html. The type context is tmp_t for files that are located at /tmp or /var/tmp. The type context used for ports on the webserver is http_port_t.

There is an SELinux policy rule in place that permits Apache, which is the webserver process running as httpd_t, to access files and directories with a context that is found in /var/ww/html and other web server directories(httpd_ssy_content_t). Files that are found in the /tmp or /var/tmp have a no allow rule in the SELinux policy, and therefore no access is allowed. A malicious user cannot access the /tmp directory with the presence of SELinux. SELinux has rules for even remote file systems such as CIFS and NFS, although every file has the same context on these file systems.

The SELinux context set on files and directories can be viewed using the most common commands along with the -Z option. Commands like ps, cp, ls, and mkdir can all use the -Z option to set or display the SELinux contexts.

Modes in SELinux

There are times when you will need to troubleshoot issues, and SELinux protection needs to be temporarily disabled for this purpose. This is achieved by using SELinux modes. There are three modes of SELinux security.

- Enforcing mode

- Permissive mode

- Disabled mode

In enforcing mode, SELinux will not allow any access to the files and directory having the context tmp_t on the webserver. The SELinux security both protects and logs while enforcing more.

The permissive mode comes into the picture mostly while troubleshooting issues. All interactions are allowed in permissive mode, even if there are no explicit rules. All interactions which would be blocked otherwise in enforcing more are logged in permissive mode. The content that is usually restricted by SELinux can be given temporary access in permissive mode. There is no need for rebooting the system when switching between enforcing and permissive modes.

The third mode is known as disabled, where SELinux security is disabled completely. To disable SELinux altogether, you will need to reboot the system. A system reboot is also required to switch from disabled mode to any other mode.

Using permissive mode in SELinux is preferred over disabling it altogether. This is because the Linux kernel still maintains the SELinux file systems even in permissive mode. This helps prevent the unnecessary relabeling of the file system when the system goes through a reboot when SELinux is enabled.

You can use the getenforce command to display the current mode of SELinux in effect.

[root@server~]]# getenforce

Enforcing

Booleans in SELinux

There are switches in Linux which help change the SELinux policy, known as SELinux booleans. SELinux booleans are rules which a system admin can enable or disable. Security admins also use it to fine-tune the security by making selective adjustments to the policy.

The getsebool command displays the SELinux booleans and their current value. A list of all the booleans can be displayed using the -a option.

[root@server~]# getsebool -a

abrt_anon_write → off

allow_console_login → on

allow_corosync_tw_tmpfs → off

Changing the Modes of SELinux

In this section, we will learn how to change the current SELinux mode in a system and to set the default SELinux mode in a system.

You can disable SELinux temporarily for purposes of troubleshooting, with the help of SELinux modes. In this section, we will learn how switching between SELinux enforcing and permissive modes can be helpful. We will also learn how to set the default mode for SELinux, which is triggered during system boot.

Changing the Current Mode of SELinux

You can modify the current SELinux mode by using the setenforce command.

[root@server~]# getenforce

Enforcing

[root@server~]# setenforce

usage: setenforce [Enforcing | Permissive | 1 | 0]

[root@server~]# setenforce 0

[root@server~]# getenforce

Permissive

[root@server~]# setenforce Enforcing

[root@server~]# getenforce

Enforcing

You can also pass a parameter to the kernel at boot time to set the mode of SELinux temporarily. You can pass a kernel argument of enforcing=0, which will boot the system in the permissive move. If you pass a kernel argument of 1, the system will boot in enforcing mode. If you pass the selinux=0 parameter to the kernel, the system will have SELinux mode disabled during boot time.

Setting the Default Mode of SELinux

This can be done by setting up the boot time configuration for SELinux in the file at /etc/SELinux/config. The following line in the configuration file determines the default SELinux mode at boot time.

SELINUX=

You can set this to enforcing, permissive, or disabled.

This is how you can use the /etc/SELinux/config file to set the default SELinux mode during boot time. The configuration file for SELinux in the older versions of Red Hat Enterprise Linux was set in a file located at /etc/sysconfig/SELinux. This file is just a symbolic link pointing to /etc/SELinux/config in Red Hat Enterprise Linux 7.

Changing Contexts of SELinux

In this section, we will learn to set the SELinux security context of files that are a part of the policy and also how to restore the SELinux security context of a file.

Initial SELinux Context

The initial SELinux context is determined by the SELinux context of its parent directory. The newly created file is assigned the context of its parent directory. This works for common commands like cp, touch, and vim. However, if a file is created in a different location where permissions are retained using commands like mv or cp, the original SELinux context remains unchanged.

Changing the SELinux Context for a File

There are two commands available in Red Hat Enterprise Linux to change the SELinux context of a file: restorecon and chcon. An argument can be supplied to the chcon command to change the context of a file. Most times, the -t option is specified only to change the type context of the file.

The first choice of command to change the SELinux context of a file or directory is retorecon. There is no need to explicitly pass the context while using the restorecon command, as in chcon. It automatically sets the context of the file by checking the rules in the SELinux policy.

Note: Ideally speaking, it is not advisable to use the chcon command to change the SELinux context of files. There is scope for mistakes when you are manually specifying the context. If the file systems are relabeled at boot time, the context of the files is reverted to their default contexts.

Changing booleans of SELinux

In this section, we will learn how to make adjustments to the behavior of a policy by making changes to the SELinux booleans.

SELinux booleans

The switches that can change the behavior of SELinux policies are known as SELinux booleans. They are rules which can be either enabled or disabled. Security admin can use SELinux booleans to make selective adjustments by fine-tuning policies.

There are many manual pages available in the SELinux-policy-devel package, which will give an elaborate description of booleans and how they can be used with various services. If the package is installed, you can use the man -k '_selinux' command to list all the documents on SELinux booleans.

The SELinux booleans can be viewed by using the getsebool command, and they can be modified using the setsebool command. The modification on the boolean can be made persistent by using the setsebool -P command. If you want to verify whether a boolean is persistent or not along with a small description, you can use the semanage setsebool -l command.

[root@server~]# getsebool -a

abrt_anon_write → off

abrt_handle_event → off

abrt_upload_watch_anon_write → on

antivirus_can_scan_system → off

antivirus_use_jit → off

Troubleshooting Issues in SELinux

In this section, we will learn about the log analysis tools available in SELinux.

There will be times when you will be stuck as SELinux will prevent access to certain files on the server. There are a few steps that you can take as a system admin to solve this issue.

- Before trying to make any changes or modifications, you may want to consider that SELinux is doing the right thing by preventing access to a file. If a web server is trying to gain access to the /home directory, it will imply a compromise of the service if there are no web files present in that directory. If there are web files in this directory and access is necessary, then additional steps would be needed.

- Incorrect context on a file is one of the most common reasons for an SELinux issue. This can be expected if the context on a file was one thing during its creation, and then changed when it got moved to another location. The easiest solution would be to run restorecon on such a file. Using restorecon will also ensure that there is no impact on the other files and their security in the system.

- You can also modify a boolean to correct or modify the access that is too restrictive.

- You cannot rule out the possibility of a bug in the SELinux system, which is causing access issues. Although there have been a lot of upgrades to SELinux and this is a very rate event. If you are sure that there is a bug in the SELinux system, you can call Red Hat support to report the issue so that they can fix the bug as soon as possible.

CHAPTER 8

◆·+————————◆·+·◆·+·◆————————+·◆

Network Defined Users and Groups

The objective of this chapter is to configure a system through which identities can be managed centrally. We will be learning about how we can connect to users and groups that are defined by the network.

- Identity management services

- Authentication services and user information

- Need for centralized identity management

In the modern era, there are multiple systems connected through a network that have various services running on them. There will be users that will be using these systems, and keeping their accounts local to the machine can be a tedious task as you will have to configure those users on every system. If the same user needs to be given access to multiple machines, you will need to ensure that the user has been created on every machine, and the password is synchronized through all those machines.

A solution to this challenge is that we do not store the user accounts and their passwords locally. This information is stored on a central system from where it can be retrieved through other systems on the network the systems are connected to. Having all the user information and authentication information stored centrally also makes way for something known as a Single Sign-On (SSO). A single sign-on is a method through which a user only needs to authenticate themselves once using their password on one service. Then a token or cookie is obtained through which authentication is done automatically for all other services.

User Information and Authentication

The following two services are essential for a central identity management system.

- Account Information: The information such as username, location of the home directory, group memberships, UID, GID, etc. fall under this service. There are popular solutions like IPA server, Network Information Services NIS, and Active Directory, which make use of LDAP (Lightweight Directory Access Protocol) for storing account information.

- Authentication Information: This is a method through which a system can validate a user is who they claim to be. This is achieved by sending an encrypted password to the server or by providing a cryptographic password hash to the client system. An LDAP server is popular for this as it can provide authentication information in addition to account information. Another service is known as Kerberos only provides single sign-on authentication services, and is usually combined with LDAP for account information. Active Directory and IPA server both use Kerberos.

In Red Hat Enterprise Linux 7, the /etc/passwd file store local information of users, while the /etc/shadow file store authentication information of users in a hashed format.

Connecting a System to Centralized LDAP and Kerberos Servers

Authconfig

If you wish to configure a Red Hat Enterprise Linux 7 system to use centralized identity management, various configuration files need to be modified, along with the configuration of a few daemons as well. You will need to at least modify the following files to connect your Red Hat Enterprise Linux system to a centralized LDAP and Kerberos server.

- /etc/ldap.conf: The information for the central LDAP server will be specified in this file.

- /etc/krb5.conf: The information for the central Kerberos server will be specified in this file.

- /etc/sssd/sssd.conf: The system security services daemon is configured using this file. This daemon is usually used for caching information of the user and user authentication info.

- /etc/nsswitch.conf: This configuration in this file indicates which authentication services and user information should be used to the system.

- /etc/pam.d/*: This file configures how authentication is managed for various services.

- /etc/openldap/cacerts: CA certificates are root certificate authorities used to validate SSL certificates, which are used to validate LDAP servers.

It is important to enable and start the sssd daemon before the system can use it.

It is very easy to make a mistake when you have so many files and services to configure. There is a set of tools to automate these configurations in Red Hat Enterprise Linux 7. Authconfig.authconfig comes with three tools that are capable of performing all these configurations.

authconfig

This is a command-line tool. Configurations across multiple systems can be automated using this tool. The commands used with authconfig are very long as they have numerous parameters to be passed with them. The tool is installed as a part of the authconfig package.

authconfig-tui

This is an interactive version of the authconfig tool. It comes with a menu-driven text interface. It is possible to use this tool with ssh as well. The tool is installed as a part of the authconfig package.

authconfig-gtk

This is a graphical version of the authconfig. It can also be launched as system-config-authentication. The tool is installed as a part of the authconfig-gtk package.

Important LDAP Parameters

There are various settings for authconfig so that we can connect it to the central LDAP server to fetch user information.

- You will need to specify the hostname of the LDAP server

- The base DN(Distinguished Name) of the part of the LDAP tree where the system should be searching for user information. The syntax of this is something like

  dc=example, dc=com

OR

ou=People, =-PonyCorp

The server admin for the LDAP server should be able to provide this information to you.

- If communication with the LDAP server is secured through TLS or SSL, The LDAP server will provide a root CA certificate that is responsible for the validation of the SSL certificate.

Note: The system needs extra packages installed as well so that it can provide the functionality of an LDAP client. All the necessary dependencies can be installed by installing sssd.

Important Kerberos Parameters

There are various settings for authconfig so that we can connect it to the central Kerberos server to fetch user authentication information.

1. The Kerberos realm name to be used. A Kerberos realm is a domain of machines that all use a standard set of Kerberos servers and users for authentication.

2. There are one or more key distribution centers KDC required. This will be the hostname for the Kerberos server.

3. The hostname of one or more admin servers. This is the machine that clients communicate with when there is a change in password or other modifications are required. Ideally, this machine is the same as the primary key distribution center but can be a different machine as well.

In addition to this, a system administrator can define if there is a DNS lookup needed to look up for the realm to be used for a particular hostname. The DNS lookup can also help to find a key distribution center and other admin servers automatically. Issues related to Kerberos can be debugged by installing one extra package. This package also helps you to work with Kerberos tickets through the command line. The package is known as the krb5-workstation.

Using authconfig-gtk

As discussed, you can use authconfig-gtk, which is a graphical interface to configure your system to connect to an LDAP or Kerberos server. You can use the following steps to configure.

- Install all the necessary packages to use authconfig-gtk

  [user@desktop~]$ sudo yum -y install authconfig-gtk sssd krb5-workstation

- You can now launch authconfig-gtk from the command line or Applications>>Sundry>>Authentication. You will need to enter the root password if you are prompted for it.

- A window for authconfig will popup. On the tab for Identity and Authentication, select LDAP on the dropdown for User Account Database. Fill the fields for LDAP Search Base DN and LDAP server fields using the information given by the LDAP server admin.

- Check the box for Use TLS to encrypt the connections box if your LDAP server supports TLS. Next, you can use the Download CA Certificate button to download the root CA certificate.

- In the dropdown for Authentication Method, select Kerberos Password. Fill out the details for Kerberos realm, admin servers, Key Distribution Center KDC, in their respective fields. These will be provided to you by the Kerberos server admin.

- If there are no central home directories created, users will be able to create them on the first login if the Create home directories on the first login box are checked on the Advanced Options tab.

- Save and activate all the changes by hitting the apply button. The changes will be written automatically to all configuration files, and the sssd service will be restarted.

Testing the Configuration

The test for the LDAP + Kerberos configuration is simple. A system admin can use ssh to login to the system using the login credentials of any network user. Additionally, the gretent command can be used to fetch information of a network user using the following syntax.

gretent passwd <USERNAME>

Note: If the configuration is default, the sssd service will not enumerate network users if the username is not passed with the gretent command. This is done so that the graphical login screen is not cluttered and also such that time and network resources are not wasted.

Connecting a System to an IPA Server

There is an integrated service provided by Red Hat Enterprise Linux to configure LDAP and Kerberos, known as an IPA server. IPA stands for Identity, Policy, and Auditing. An IPA server provides a set of command-line and web-based administration tools to both LDAP and Kerberos. In addition to user information and authentication information, IPA can centralize other things such as sudo rules, SSH host keys, SSH public keys, TLS certificates, maps for automounting, and much more.

Using ipa-client

As already discussed, we can use the authconfig tool to configure a Red Hat Enterprise Linux system to use an IPA server. Still, there are specialized tools available, too, such as the IPA-client-install. The command is a part of the IPA-client package, which will include all other dependencies such as sssd.

The significant benefit of using the IPA-client-install is that it is capable of pulling all necessary information automatically from DNS in both cases where the IPA server configures it or configured manually by a system admin. It can also create host entries and more on the IPA server. Given this, the policies for a host can be accessed by a server admin.

If the IPA-client-install tool is run without passing any arguments, by default, it tries to pull information about the IPA server for its DNS domain from DNS. If that fails, the admin will then be prompted to provide necessary information such as the realm to use and the domain name of the IPA server. Other information includes the username and password of the account that is allowed to create new machine entries on the IPA server. If there is no exclusive account created for this job, the default account of the IPA server administrator (admin) can be used for this as well.

Connecting a System to Active Directory

There are multiple methods available in Red Hat Enterprise Linux 7 to join the system to an Active Directory. As a system admin, you can install the samba-winbind package. You can configure winbind through the tools available in the family of authconfig. Alternatively, the system admin can install the realmd and sssd packages so that they can use the realm and sssd commands.

Note: You can use the realm command to connect to Kerberos realms or IPA server domains. However, the final configuration is a bit different.

For example, there will be @domain appended to the username for users. Therefore, to join the IPA domains, it is advisable to use the IPA-client-install method.

Let us go through an example where we will use realmd to join an Active Directory Domain, where we will allow users of the Active Directory to log into the local system. In the example, we assume that the active directory domain is called domain.example.com.

- You will need to install all the relevant packages. Mostly realmd.

  [user@desktop~]$ yum -y install realmd

- The next step is the discovery of settings for your domain.

  [user@desktop~]$ sudo realm discover domain.example.com

- The next step is to join the domain for Active Directory. This will automatically install all dependencies as well, namely, pam, sssd, /etc/nsswitch.conf, etc.

  [user@desktop~]$ sudo realm join domain.example.com

- This step will try to join the local system to the Active directory using the account of the administrator. If prompted to enter the administrator's password, enter it. You can pass the --user argument if you wish to use any account other than the administrator.

- Accounts connected to the Active Directory can now be used on the system. However, you still won't be able to login using Active Directory. You can enable logins using the following commands.

  [user@desktop~]$ sudo realm permit --realm domain.example.com --all

- If you wish only to allow a select number of users, you can replace --all with a list of users, as shown in the command below.

  [user@desktop~]$ sudo realm permit --realm domain.example.com DOMAIN\\Itchy DOMAIN\\Scratchy

CHAPTER 9

Disk Partitions and File Systems

The goal of this chapter is to learn how to create and manage disks and their partitions, and file systems using the command line. We will learn how to create simple disk partitions and file systems. We will also learn about the swap and how to manage swap space.

Partitions, File Systems, and Mounting

The objectives of this section are as follows.

- Use fdisk to create and delete partitions on a disk that have the MBR scheme for partitioning;

- Use gdisk to create and delete partitions on a disk that have the GPT scheme for partitioning;

- Use mkfs to format file systems on devices;

- Mount file systems to the directory tree.

Disk Partitioning

When you use the disk partitioning technology, a physical hard drive can be divided into multiple logical storage units known as partitions. The motive to divide a disk into multiple partitions is to use the partitions on a physical disk for various functions. Let us go through a few examples where partitioning proves to be necessary and beneficial.

- When you want to limit the amount of space provided to a user or an application;

- When you wish to install multiple operating systems on the same physical disk so that you can use multiple systems on the same machine;

- Create a boundary between the files for an operating system or programs, and that for a user;

- Create some extra space for virtual memory swapping of the operating system;

- Create a limit on the actual disk space available to users so that there is a space of backups and diagnostic tools.

MBR Partitioning Scheme

Since 1982, the Master Boot Record or MBR partitioning scheme has dominated the disk partitioning methods for systems that run on BIOS firmware. There is a maximum of four primary partitions that are supported by this scheme. However, on a Linux system, a system admin can create up to 15 partitions using extended and logical partitions. The system uses 32-bit values to store partition data. Therefore disks that are partitioned using the MBR scheme can have a maximum disk and partition size of 2 TiB.

However, in today's world, we know that disk sizes go way beyond 2 TiB. Therefore, using an MBR scheme for partitioning is a challenge. It is no longer a theoretical limit, but a huge problem faced in production environments. Given this, the MBR partitioning scheme is in the process of being deprecated. It will be replaced by the GUID Partition Table, also known as GPT.

GPT Partitioning Scheme

The GPT partition table is used on physical hard disks of systems that run on the Unified Firmware Interface or known as the UEFI firmware. The GPT system overcomes many of the limitations faced by the MBR scheme. The GPT table can support the creation of up to 128 partitions as per the UEFI specifications. Unlike the MBR scheme, which uses 32 bits for storing information related to size and logical block addresses, the GPT system uses 64 bits for storing logical block addresses. Given this, GPT can create partitions on disks with size up to 8 zebibyte ZiB, or 8 billion tebibytes.

In addition to overcoming challenges faced by the MBR partitioning scheme, there are a few additional features and benefits offered by the GPT partition table. GPT can uniquely identify each disk and partition since it uses 128-bit GUIDs. MBR has a single point of failure. In contrast to this, GPT has redundancy for its partition table information. There is a primary GPT that is placed at the beginning of the disk, and in case of failure, there is a secondary GPT present at the end of the disk. GPT also has CRC checksum methods to detect corruption or errors in the partition table or the GPT header.

Using fdisk to Manage MBR Partitions

Partition editors are applications that can be used by system admins to make changes to the partitions on the disk. Using partition editors, system admins can perform actions such as the creation of partitions, deletion of partitions, and changing the type of partition. The fdisk partition editor is popular for disks with the MBR partitioning scheme, and all these operations are supported by fdisk.

Creating MBR Partitions

There are eight steps involved in the process of creating MBR partitions.

Select The Device Or Disk For Partition

You will need to be logged in as the root user to use the fdisk command. Execute the fdisk command as the root user and pass the name of the disk device as an argument. The fdisk command will be launched in the interactive mode, and you will have a command prompt at hand.

[root@desktop~]# fdisk /dev/vda

Welcome to fdisk

Changes will remain in memory only until you decide to write them.

Be careful before using the write command.

Command (m for help):

Request A New Primary Or Extended Partition

You can enter the n key on the keyboard to request a new partition. You will need to specify whether the partition should be a primary partition or an extended partition. By default, a primary partition is taken into consideration.

Partition type:

p   primary(0 primary, 0 extended, 4 free)

e   extended

Select (default p): p

Note: If you need to create more than four partitions, you can do so by creating three primary partitions and one extended partition. The extended partition will act as a container on which you can create many other logical partitions.

Specify The Partition Numbers

The partition number serves as an identifier for the partition on the disk, which is used for any future operations to be performed on the partition. By default, it takes the lowest unused value.

Partition number (1-4, default 1): 1

Define Where The Partition Begins

By default, this value is the first available sector on the disk.

First sector (2048-20971519, default 2048): 2048

Define Where The Partition Should End

By default, this value will end at the first sector of the next partition on the disk or the actual last sector of the disk.

Last sector, +sectors or +size{K, M, G} (6144-20971519, default 20971519): 1056739

In addition to specifying the sector number, fdisk also allows you to enter the size of the partition in KiB, MiB, or GiB. On using this, the end sector will be calculated automatically.

After you have entered the boundary for a sector, a confirmation for the partition creation is displayed by fdisk.

Partition 1 of type Linux and size 1024 MiB is set.

Define The Partition Type

By default, the type for the partition is Linux. If you wish to use another type for the partition, you can use the t command to change the partition type. You will be prompted to enter the hex code for the new partition type. You can use the L command to display the hex code for each partition type. It is critical to set the right type of partitions because of compatibility with using certain tools. For example, when the Linux kernel comes across a partition type of 0xfd, Linux RAID, it will attempt to autostart the RAID volume.

Command (m for help): t

Selected partition 1

Hex code (type L to list all codes): 82

Changed type of partition 'Linux' to 'Linux swap / Solaris.'

Make a Note Of The Changes Made

You can write the changes made to the partition table by using the w command. Make sure you have verified everything before writing the changes. The w command will write all changes and exit the fdisk program immediately.

Command (m for help): w

The partition table has been altered!

Calling ioctl() to re-read partition table.

Warning: Re-reading the partition failed with error 16: Device or resource busy.

The kernel still uses the old table. The new table will be used at the next reboot or after you run partprobe or kpartx.

Syncing disks.

Re-Read The New Partition Table

Execute the partprobe command by passing the disk device name as an argument to force a re-read of the partition table.

[root@desktop~]# partprobe /dev/vda

Note: When you use fdisk, all the edits you make to the partition table are stored in memory and are only written to the disks when you use the w command, which will write all the changes to the disk. If you do not use the w command before exiting the fdisk program, the changes will be discarded, and the partition table of the disk will remain the same. This is a useful feature in case a system admin issues unwanted changes to the fdisk programs. To discard instructions given to fdisk, exit the fdisk program without saving the changes.

Removing MBR Partitions

There are five steps in fdisk to delete a partition from a disk that uses the MBR partitioning.

Specify the Disk Where You Need To Delete The Partition

Execute the fdisk command and pass the disk device name as an argument.

[root@desktop~]# fdisk /dev/vda

Welcome to fdisk

Changes will remain in memory only until you decide to write them.

Be careful before using the write command.

Command (m for help):

Identify The Partition Number That You Want To Delete

You can use the p command in fdisk to print the partition table, which will give you the partitions created with the disk device name.

Command (m for help): p

Request To Delete The Partition

You can use the d command to request the partition to be deleted by specifying the partition number.

Command (m for help): d

Selected partition 1

Partition 1 is deleted

Save The Changes Made

As already discussed, use the w command to save the changes that you have made to the partition table.

Command (m for help): w

The partition table has been altered!

Calling ioctl() to re-read partition table.

Warning: Re-reading the partition failed with error 16: Device or resource busy.

The kernel still uses the old table. The new table will be used at the next reboot or after you run partprobe or kpartx.

Syncing disks.

Ensure The Kernel Reads The New Partition Table

You can use the partprobe command to force the kernel to re-read the changes made to the partition table without needing to reboot the system.

[root@desktop~]# partprobe /dev/vda

GPT partitions

The gdisk partition editor is popular for disks with the GPT partitioning scheme, and all these operations are supported by gdisk.

Note: Support for GPT partitioning has been added to fdisk as well, but it is experimental. So it would be safe to say that gdisk is the command to be used to work with disk partitioning using the GPT partitioning scheme.

Creating GPT Partitions

You can create a GPT partition using the eight steps given below.

Specify the Disk Or Device To Create The Partition

On the command line, use the gdisk command and pass the disk device that you want to partition as an argument to the command. The gdisk command will commence an interactive mode, and you will be presented with a command prompt.

[root@desktop~]# gdisk /dev/vda

GPT fdisk (gdisk) version 0.8.6

Partition table scan:

MBR: not present

BSD: not present

APM: not present

GPT: not present

Creating new GPT entries.

Command (? for help):

Request A New Partition

You can enter n on the command prompt to create a new partition.

Command (? for help): n

Specify The Number To Be Assigned To The Partition

The partition number serves as an identifier for the partition on the disk. This partition will be used for any future operations to be performed on the partition. By default, it takes the lowest unused value.

Partition number (1-128, default 1): 1

Specify Where The Partition Should Start

There are two inputs supported by gdisk for disk location. The first type of input is where you specify the absolute number of the disk sector, which will be the first sector of the new partition.

First sector (34-20971486, default = 2048) or {+-}size{KMGTP}: 2048

The second type of input is one that specifies the starting point of the partition about the first or the last sector of the first contiguous block of free sectors on the disk. You can provide input in units such as KiB, MiB, GiB, TiB, or PiB using the second type of input.

For example, if you specify the input as 256 MiB, the partition will be created for 256 MiB after the next group of contiguous available sectors. On the other hand, if you specify a value of negative -256 MiB, it would imply a sector located 256 MiB before the available contiguous sectors.

Define Where The Partition Should End

By default, this value will be the last sector of the available contiguous sectors, which are still unallocated.

Last sector (2048-20971486, default = 20971486) or {+-}size{KMGTP}: 1067834

Again like the first sector, you can provide a size for the last sector where it should end. You can provide input in units such as KiB, MiB, GiB, TiB, or PiB using the second type of input.

Last sector (2048-20971486, default = 20971486) or {+-}size{KMGTP}: +256M

On the other hand, if you specify a value of negative -256 MiB, it would imply a sector located 256 MiB before the end of available contiguous sectors.

Last sector (2048-20971486, default = 20971486) or {+-}size{KMGTP}: -256M

Define The Partition Type

The partition type is Linux, by default, for partitions created using the gdisk command. You will need to enter the corresponding hex code if you wish to define a different type of partition. You can use the L command to display a list of hex commands if you do not know the codes.

Current type is 'Linux filesystem'

Hex code or GUID (L to show codes, Enter = 8300): 8e00

Changed type of partition to 'Linux LVM'

Save The Changes Made

The w command, just like in fdisk is used in gdisk to write all the changes made to the partition table. Enter y when gdisk prompts you for final confirmation.

Command (? for help): w

Final checks complete. About to write GPT data. THIS WILL OVERWRITE EXISTING PARTITIONS!!

Do you want to proceed? (Y/N): y

OK; writing new GUID partition table (GPT) to /dev/vda.

The operation has completed successfully.

Force The Kernel To Read The Partition

Execute the partprobe command by passing the disk device name as an argument to force a re-read of the partition table.

[root@desktop~]# partprobe /dev/vda

Note: When you use gdisk, all the edits you make to the partition table are stored in memory and are only written to the disks when you use the w command, which will write all the changes to the disk. If you do not use the w command before exiting the gdisk program, the changes will be discarded, and the partition table of the disk will remain the same. This is a useful feature in case a system admin issues unwanted changes to the gdisk programs. To discard instructions given to gdisk, exit the gdisk program without saving the changes.

Deleting or Removing GPT Disk Partitions

You can remove a partition using gdisk in the GPT partitioning scheme using five steps as given below.

Specify the Device Where You Want To Delete The Partition

Use the gdisk command to pass the disk device as an argument on which you need to work.

[root@desktop~]# gdisk /dev/vda

GPT fdisk (gdisk) version 0.8.6

Partition table scan:

MBR: not present

BSD: not present

APM: not present

GPT: present

Found valid GPT with protective MBR; using GPT.

Command (? for help):

Identify Where The Partition Should Be Deleted

You can print the partition table by entering p. The number field will show the partition number for a given partition.

Number	Start sector	End sector	Size	Code	Name
1	2048	1050623	256 MiB	8E00	Linux LVM

Setup The Partition Deletion

You can initiate a deletion or removal of partition by entering the d command.

Command (? for help): d

Using 1

Save The Changes Made To The Disk

The w command, just like in fdisk, is used in gdisk to write all the changes made to the partition table. Enter y when gdisk prompts you for final confirmation.

Command (? for help): w

Final checks complete. About to write GPT data. THIS WILL OVERWRITE EXISTING PARTITIONS!!

Do you want to proceed? (Y/N): y

OK; writing new GUID partition table (GPT) to /dev/vda.

The operation has completed successfully.

Force The Kernel To Re-Read Partition Made

Execute the partprobe command by passing the disk device name as an argument to force a re-read of the partition table.

[root@desktop~]# partprobe /dev/vda

File System Creation

After the creation of a block device, your next steps should be to apply a file system to it. The motive of applying a file system to a block device is so that the block can be structures, and data can be written to it or retrieved from it. There are different types of file systems supported on Red Hat Enterprise Linux. However, there are two common file systems, which are xfs and ext4. The anaconda installer for Red Hat Enterprise Linux uses the xfs file system by default.

A file system can be applied to a block device by using the mkfs command. If you do not specify the file system to be used, the ext2 file system will be applied by default. Note that ext2 is not desirable for multiple applications. You can pass the -t option to specify the file system.

[root@desktop~]# mkfs -t xfs /dev/vda1

File System Mounting

After you have applied the file system to a block device, your final step to add the new file system is to attach it to the directory structure. Once the file system gets added to the directory structure, user space utilities can access it to write data to it or retrieve data from it.

Manual Mounting of the File System

A device can be mounted to a directory location or mount point manually by using the mount command. Using the mount command, you will need to specify the mount point and the device to be mounted. You can pass additional options along with the command if desired to assign custom behavior to the device.

[root@desktop~]# mount /dev/vda1 /mnt

You can view the list of currently mounted directories, mount points and other options using the mount command as well.

It is an excellent way to check if a file system that was created is working in the way it was intended to by manually mounting it. However, a manual mount is not retained across system reboots. Once you reboot the system, the mount point will be removed from the directory tree. If you want a mount point to be permanently mounted to the directory tree, you will need to add a listing for the file system to eh file located at /etc/fstab.

Persistently Mounting File Systems

Once you add an entry for a file system in the /etc/fstab file, you can ensure that a device is mounted to the directory tree across system reboots.

There are six fields per line in the /etc/fstab file.

In the first field, the device to be used is specified. This could be the UUID of the device or the actual device file, such as /dev/vda1. A UUID is automatically generated for a file system during its creation and is stored in the file system superblock.

Note: Id is advisable to use the UUID because the block identifiers for a device can change under certain circumstances. For example, when the cloud provider changes the underlying storage layer on a virtual machine, the name of the block device may change, but the UUID is retained in the device's superblock.

The block devices on a system can be viewed using the blkid command, and the display will give you the UUID of a file system along with the format of its file system.

[root@desktop~]# blkid /dev/vda1

The second field in the fstab file shows the mount point in the directory tree where the device is mounted. The mount point shown will already exist in the system. If it does not, you can use the mkdir command to create a new mount point.

The third field of the fstab file shows the type of file system applied to the device block.

The fourth field shows the list of options to be applied to the device as a part of its custom behavior when it is mounted. This is a mandatory field. A set of options which are commonly used can be represented using the default keyword. If you want other options, you can view them in the man page of the mount command.

The dump flag and fsck order make the last two fields of the fstab file. The dump flag is used with the dump command when you need to create a backup of the contents of the device. The fsck order determines if the fsck should be run at boot time, given that the file system was not unmounted cleanly. The value of fsck shows the

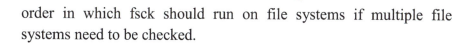

order in which fsck should run on file systems if multiple file systems need to be checked.

Note: If you have placed an invalid entry for a device in the /etc/fstab file, there are chances that the system may not boot at all. To ensure that such an event does not take place, it is your responsibility as a system admin to verify that the entries in the fstab file are valid. You can do so by unmounting the new file system followed by the mount -a command. This will read the /etc/fstab file to mount all file systems back. If the system gives an error after running the mount -a command, you need to ensure that the mistakes in the fstab file are rectified before the system is rebooted.

Swap Space Management

The objective of this section is to learn how to create and format a partition for swap space. We will also learn to activate the swap space created.

Concepts of Swap Space

An area of the disk, which can be used for memory management with the Linux kernel, is known as swap space. The objective of swap space is to hold the inactive pages of the memory when there is not enough RAM available on the system. The combination of swap space, along with system RAM, is known as virtual memory.

When the memory limit on a system is exhausted, The kernel will scan through the system RAM, searching for memory pages that are idle and assigned to processes. The kernel will release the RAM from the idle pages and allocate the swap space to such pages, in turn allocating the RAM to active processes. If a page that was assigned to the swap memory needs to be accessed by a process, it will be recalled to the RAM, and another idle page from the RAM will substitute this page in the swap memory.

Since swap space resides on the disk, the speed of swap is slow compared to RAM. It is used to help system RAM, but the use of swap space should be avoided as much as possible as it can degrade system performance.

Swap Space Creation

There are three steps involved in the creation of swap space.

1. A partition needs to be created

2. The partition type should be selected as 82 Linux Swap

3. A swap signature should be formatted on the device

Creation of the partition

You can use fdisk to create the partition and allocate the desired partition.

[root@desktop~]# fdisk /dev/vda

Welcome to fdisk

Changes will remain in memory only until you decide to write them.

Be careful before using the write command.

Command (m for help):

In the next step, you can request a new primary partition or an extended partition.

You can enter the n key on the keyboard to request a new partition. You will need to specify whether the partition should be a primary partition or an extended partition. By default, a primary partition is taken into consideration.

Partition type:

p   primary(0 primary, 0 extended, 4 free)

e   extended

Select (default p): p

Note: If you need to create more than four partitions, you can do so by creating three primary partitions and one extended partition. The extended partition will act as a container on which you can create many other logical partitions.

Specify a number for the partition

The partition number serves as an identifier for the partition on the disk, which is used for any future operations to be performed on the partition. By default, it takes the lowest unused value.

Partition number (1-4, default 1): 1

Define the first sector of the disk where the partition will begin.

By default, this value is the first available sector on the disk.

First sector (2048-20971519, default 2048): 2048

Define the last sector of the disk where you want the current partition to end.

By default, this value will end at the first sector of the next partition on the disk or the actual last sector of the disk.

Last sector, +sectors or +size{K, M, G} (6144-20971519, default 20971519): 1056739

In addition to specifying the sector number, fdisk also allows you to enter the size of the partition in KiB, MiB, or GiB. On using this, the end sector will be calculated automatically.

After you have entered the boundary for a sector, a confirmation for the partition creation is displayed by fdisk.

Partition 1 of type Linux and size 1024 MiB is set.

Assign the type of partition

The next step is to change the type of partition to Linux Swap.

By default, the type for the partition is Linux. If you wish to use another type for the partition, you can use the t command to change the partition type. You will be prompted to enter the hex code for the new partition type. You can use the L command to display the hex code for each partition type. It is critical to set the right type of partitions because of compatibility with using specific tools. For example, when the Linux kernel comes across a partition type of 0xfd, Linux RAID, it will attempt to autostart the RAID volume. Since the partition hex code for Linux Swap is 82, we will be assigning the partition type hex code as 82.

Command (m for help): t

Selected partition 1

Hex code (type L to list all codes): 82

Changed type of partition 'Linux' to 'Linux swap / Solaris'

Formatting the Created Device

You can apply a swap signature to the device by using the mkswap command. As opposed to other formatting tools, mkswap will write a single block of data to the start of the device, without formatting the rest of the device so that it can store memory pages.

[root@desktop~]# mkswap /dev/vda1

Activating the Swap Space

As a system admin, you can use the swapon command to activate the swap space that you just created and formatted. You can pass the device as an argument to the swapon command, or you can use the swapon -a command which will activate all the swap spaces defined in the /etc/fstab file.

[root@desktop~]# free

[root@desktop~]# swapon /dev/vda1

Activating the Swap Space Permanently

As we have already seen, the partition for swap space will not be retained if the system goes through a reboot. You will need to add the partition to the /etc/fstab file so that it is retained across reboots.

You can also deactivate a swap space by using the swapoff command. The swapoff command will only be successful if there are alternative swap spaces available to write the pages from a particular swap space or if they can be written back to the system RAM. The swapoff command will fail if there are no swap spaces available where the data can be written. You will get an error prompt, and the current swap space will remain active.

CHAPTER 10

————•+•——•+•+•+•——•+•————

Logical Volume Management

In this system, we will learn how to use the command line to manage logical volumes. We will learn about the components involved in logical volume management. We will further learn how to manage logical volumes and extend logical volumes further.

Logical Volume Management Concepts

By the end of this section, you will be in a position to describe the components of Logical Volume Management.

Concepts

Disk space can be managed more efficiently using logical volumes and logical volume management. If the space requirement is high for a file system hosted in an LVM, it can be easily allocated to its logical volume from the available free space in its volume group. This can be achieved by resizing the file system. You can also add a physical disk as replacement if a disk fails. The new physical disk can be added as a logical volume to the file system, and the logical volume's extents can be added to the new disk.

Logical Volume Management Definitions

- Physical devices are storage devices which are used to store data permanently in a logical volume. Physical devices are block-based devices, which can be whole disks, disk partitions, RAID arrays, or Storage Area Network SAN disks. If you want to use a device with LVM, you will need to initialize that device as a physical volume for LVM. The entire device will be considered to be a physical volume.

- Physical Volumes PV register the physical devices that lie below and are to be used in volume groups. Physical devices PE are automatically segmented into Physical Extents PE by LVM. They are ideally small blocks of data that act as the smallest block of storage on a PV.

- Volume Groups VG are pools of storage which consist of one or more physical volumes. A physical volume PV can be allocated single volume group VG only. There can be any number of logical volumes or unused space residing on a volume group.

- Logical Volumes LV are a result of free physical extents in a volume group. They provide storage devices which are used by users, applications, and the operating system. Logical volumes are a collection of logical extents, which are mapped to physical extents, the smallest part of storage on a physical volume. The default behavior is for every logical extent to map to one physical extent. This default mapping behavior can be changed by changing the specific settings for a logical volume. For example, in the case of mirroring, every logical extent is mapped to two physical extents.

Logical Volume Management

The objective of this section is to implement LVM storage and display the component information for LVM.

LVM Storage Implementation

There is an elaborate set of command-line tools available for LVM. These tools can be used for the implementation and management of LVM storage. The command-line tools can be combined with scripts to implement automation.

Note: The examples that follow will consider the vda device and its partitions to display the use of commands in LVM. In the real world, you will need to ensure that you choose the correct device for the disk and its partitions, which are a part of your system.

Creating a Logical Volume

A usable logical volume can be created in five steps.

Prepare A Physical Device

A partition needs to be created to be used with LVM. You can use tools such as fdisk, gdisk, or parted to create the required partition. When you have to define the type of partition, make sure you select Linux LVM. You can use the hex code 0x8e in MBR partitions. You will also need to ensure to use the partprobe command in the end so that the changes to the partition table are registered to the system kernel.

As an alternative, you can also use a whole disk, a RAID array, or a Storage Area Network SAN disk.

You need to prepare a physical device only if no physical disk is already prepared, and you need a new physical volume to create or extend a volume group.

[root@desktop~]# fdisk /dev/vda

As discussed in the previous chapter, you can use m for help, p to print the partition table, n to create a new partition, t to define the partition type, w to save the changes made to the partition table, and q to quit.

Create A Physical Volume

You can use the pvcreate command in LVM to give a label to a partition to be used as a physical volume. The LVM configuration data will be saved to the physical volume directly through a header. A physical volume is divided into physical extents of the same size, for example, 8 MiB blocks. You can pass space-delimited device names as arguments to the pvcreate command to create several devices at the same time.

[root@desktop~]# pvcreate /dev/vda2 /dev/vdb1

Using this command, you will be able to give physical volume labels to the devices at /dev/vda1 and /dev/vdb2. This will make these devices ready to be allocated in a volume group.

Create A Volume Group

The command vgcreate available in LVM is used to create a pool of one or more physical volumes, known as a volume group. The number of physical extents available in the pool determines the size of the volume group. A volume group will host one or more logical volumes. This is achieved by allocating free physical extents to a logical volume. Therefore, at the time of the creation of a logical volume, a sufficient number of physical extents must be free and available.

You will need to pass a name for the volume group and one or more physical volumes as arguments to the vgcreate command to create a volume group.

[root@desktop~]# vgcreate vgone /dev/vda2 /dev/vdb1

This will result in the creation of a volume group by the name vgone. This volume group is a combination of the sizes of the two physical volumes /dev/vda2 and /dev/vdb1.

You need to create a volume group only when no other volume group exists. It is possible to create additional volume groups if you need them for administration. Otherwise, you can extend an existing volume group to accommodate new logical volumes.

Create A Logical Volume

The lvcreate command in LVM is used to create logical volumes. It does so by using the available physical extents in a volume group. You can pass the following arguments to the lvcreate command.

-n option to give a name to the logical volume

-L to set the size of the LV in bytes along with the name of the volume group in which the logical volume is to be created

[root@desktop~]# lvcreate -n zeus -L 2G vgone

This will result in the creation of a logical volume called Zeus of size 2 GiB in the volume group vgone. You need to ensure that the volume group vgone has sufficient physical extents to allocate 2 GiB of space to the logical volume.

The size in the option -L can be specified in multiple ways. The -l option will expect an input of size measured as many physical extents.

Examples:

lvcreate -L 256M: The logical volume will be sized to a definite 256 MB

lvcreate -l 256: The logical volume will be sized to a definite 256 MB in size.

Add A File System

You will need to create an xfs file system on the newly created logical volume. You can use the mkfs command to achieve the same. You can also use any other preferred file systems such as ext4 to create the file system.

[root@desktop~]# mkfs -t xfs /dev/vgone/zeus

You will want to make this file system available across system reboots. In that case, you will need to add this file system to the /etc/fstab file. You can use the following steps to do so.

Create a Directory to Mount the File System To

[root@desktop~]# mkdir /mnt/zeus

Add an entry to the /etc/fstab file

/dev/vgone/zeus   /mnt/zeus   xfs   defaults   1 2

Execute the mount -a command to mount all the file systems to the /etc/fstab file.

[root@desktop~]# mount -a

Removing a Logical Volume

A logical volume can be removed in 4 steps.

Prepare The File System

Transfer all the data that you need to another file system. This can be followed by the umount command which will unmount the required file system. You will also need to ensure that you remove the entries associated with this file system from the /etc/fstab file.

[root@desktop~]# umount /mnt/zeus

Note: All the data present on the logical volume will be destroyed when you remove the logical volume. Therefore, it is imperative to backup or transfer your data before you begin with this process.

Remove The Logical Volume

You can use the lvremove command available in LVM to remove a logical volume when you no longer need it. You need to pass the device name as an argument.

[root@desktop~]# lvremove /dev/vgone/zeus

Ensure that you have unmounted the logical volume file system before executing this command. You will be prompted with a confirmation before removing the logical volume.

The free extents used by the logical volume will be released and can be assigned to another logical volume now.

Remove Volume Group

You can use the vgremove command in LVM to remove the volume group. You will need to pass the name of the volume group as an argument.

[root@desktop~]# vgremove vgone

The physical volumes of the volume group will be released and can now be assigned to a new volume group on the system.

Remove The Physical Volume

You can use the pvremove command available in LVM to remove physical volumes that you may no longer need. You can pass a space-delimited list of physical volume devices as an argument to remove multiple physical volumes at a time. The metadata of physical volumes will be erased from the partition. This will make the partition free so that it can be reformatted or reallocated.

[root@desktop~]# pvremove /dev/vda2 /dev/vdb1

LVM Status Review

Physical Volumes

The pvdisplay command will help you get all the information about physical volumes. If you do not pass a physical volume as an argument with the command, it will display the information of all physical volumes on the system. If you specify a device as an argument, the output will limit the information to that device.

[root@desktop~]# pvdisplay /dev/vda2

1. PV name: The first line of the output shows the name of the physical volume that is mapped to the device.

2. VG name: The second line shows the volume group to which the physical volume is allocated.

3. PV size: The third line shows the physical size of the physical volume. It also indicates any unusable space.

4. PE size: The fourth line shows the size of the physical extents.

5. Free PE: The fifth line shows the number of physical extents that are free and available to be assigned to new logical volumes.

Volume Groups

The vgdisplay command will help you to display all information related to a volume group. If you do not pass a volume group as an argument with the command, it will display the information of all volume groups on the system. If you specify a volume group name as an argument, the output will limit the information to that volume group.

[root@desktop~]# vgdisplay vgone

- VG name: The first line in the output shows the name of the volume group.

- VG size: The second line in the output shows the size of the storage pool available for the allocation of the volume group.

- Total PE: Is the number of PE units expressed in size.

- Free PE/size: Shows the total free available free space in the volume group, which can be allocated to logical volumes or to extend existing logical volumes.

Logical Volumes

The lvdisplay command will help you to display all information related to logical volumes. If you do not pass a logical volume as an argument with the command, it will display the information of all logical volumes on the system. If you specify a logical volume name as an argument, the output will limit the information to that logical volume.

[root@desktop~]# lvdisplay /dev/vgone/zeus

1. LV path: shows the name of the device for this logical volume.

2. VG name: shows the volume group to which the logical volume is allocated.

3. LV size: shows the total size of the logical volume.

4. Current LE: shows the number of logical extents used by this logical volume.

Extending Logical Volumes

The objectives of this section are as follows.

- We will be extending as well as reducing a volume group

- We will extend a logical volume which has an XFS partition

- We will extend a logical volume which has an EXT4 partition

Extending and reducing a volume group

You can add physical volumes to a volume group to add more space to it. This technique is known as extending the volume group. There will be new physical extents provided by these additional physical volumes. They can be further assigned to logical volumes.

If there are unused physical volumes, you can also remove them from a volume group. This technique is known as reducing the volume group. You can transfer data from extents of one physical volume to the extents of another physical volume using a tool called pvmove. By doing this, you will be able to add a new disk to an existing volume group, you can move data from an older or slower disk to a new disk, and you can remove the old disk from the volume group. You can perform all these tasks while a user or an application is still using the logical volumes in the volume groups.

Note: The examples that follow will consider the vdb device and its partitions to display the use of commands in LVM. In the real world, you will need to ensure that you choose the correct device for the disk and its partitions, which are a part of your system.

Extending a volume group

There are four steps involved in extending a volume group.

Prepare The Physical Device

A partition needs to be created to be used with LVM. You can use tools such as fdisk, gdisk, or parted to create the required partition. When you have to define the type of partition, make sure you select Linux LVM. You can use the hex code 0x8e in MBR partitions. You will also need to ensure to use the partprobe command in the end so that the changes to the partition table are registered to the system kernel.

As an alternative, you can also use a whole disk, a RAID array, or a Storage Area Network SAN disk.

You need to prepare a physical device only if no physical disk is already prepared, and you need a new physical volume to create or extend a volume group.

[root@desktop~]# fdisk /dev/vdb

As discussed in the previous chapter, you can use m for help, p to print the partition table, n to create a new partition, t to define the partition type, w to save the changes made to the partition table, and q to quit.

Create A Physical Volume

You can use the pvcreate command in LVM to give a label to a partition to be used as a physical volume. The LVM configuration data will be saved to the physical volume directly through a header. A physical volume is divided into physical extents of the same size, for example, 8 MiB blocks. You can pass space-delimited device names as arguments to the pvcreate command to create many devices at the same time.

[root@desktop~]# pvcreate /dev/vdb2

Using this command, you will be able to give physical volume labels to the device at /dev/vdb2. This will make this device ready to be allocated in a volume group.

Extending The Volume Group

You can use the vgextend command available in LVM to extend a volume group. You will need to pass the names of the volume group and the physical volume as arguments to this command.

[root@desktop~]# vgextend vgone /dev/vdb2

The result of this command will extend the volume group vgone by adding the size of /dev/vbd2 to it.

Verify The Additional Space

The final step is to verify if space got added to it after extending the volume group. You can use the vgdisplay command and pass the volume group as an argument to get this information. The line which contains the Free PE/size is what you need to be looking at.

[root@desktop~]# vgdisplay vgone

Reducing a Volume Group

There are only two steps involved in reducing a volume group.

Move The Physical Extents

You can use the pvmove command available in LVM to move the physical extents of a physical volume to another physical volume belonging to the volume group. You need to ensure that there are sufficient free extents available in the volume group and that they all belong to the other physical volumes.

[root@desktop~]# pvmove /dev/vdb2

This command will move the physical extents from /dev/vdb2 to other physical volumes which have available free extents in the same volume group.

Note: All the data present on the logical volume will be destroyed when you remove the logical volume. Therefore, it is crucial to backup or transfer your data before you begin with this process.

Reducing The Volume Group

You can use the vgreduce command available in LVM to reduce a volume group. You will need to pass the names of the volume group and the physical volume as arguments to this command.

[root@desktop~]# vgreduce vgone /dev/vdb2

The result of this command will reduce the volume group vgone by adding the size of /dev/vbd2 to it. As an alternative, you can also use the pvremove command if you do not wish to use the physical volume at all and want to remove it permanently.

Extending a Logical Volume in the XFS File System

One of the best features of a logical volume is that you can increase their size or capacity without having to experience any downtime. The capacity of a logical volume can be increased effortlessly by adding the free extents available in a volume group to it. This can further be used to extend the file system of the logical volume.

Extending a Logical Volume

You can extend a logical volume by following the three steps given below.

Verify If There Is Sufficient Space In The Volume Group

You can use the vgdisplay command to see if there are enough physical extents available for use.

[root@desktop~]# vgdisplay vgone

In the output of this command, check the line, which shows Free PE/size. The value of this field should show space that is equal to or more than the additional space needed. You will need to extend the volume group by the amount of space required if there is insufficient space.

Extend The Logical Volume

You can use the lvextend command to extend the logical volume. You can pass the name of the logical volume device as an argument to the command.

[root@desktop~]# lvextend -L +400M /dev/vgone/zeus

This command will increase the space of the logical volume zeus by 400 MiB.

Extend The File System

You can use the xfs_growfs /mountpoint command to extend the file system to occupy the extended logical volume. You need to ensure that the file system is in a mounted state while you run the xfs_growfs command. You will be able to use the file system even when the resize operation is being run on it.

[root@desktop~]# xfs_growfs /mnt/zeus

Note: There is a common mistake where system admins run the lvextend command but forget to run the xfs_growfs command. As an alternative, you can pass the -r argument with the lvextend command, which will run both the command consecutively. This will extend the logical volume first and then resize the file system. This support is available for various file systems.

It would be a good practice to verify the size of the new mounted file system. You can do so by running the following command.

df -h /mountpoint

Extending a Logical Volume in the EXT4 File System

Extending a Logical Volume

You can extend a logical volume by following the three steps given below.

Verify If There Is Sufficient Space In The Volume Group

You can use the vgdisplay command to see if there are enough physical extents available for use.

[root@desktop~]# vgdisplay vgone

In the output of this command, check the line, which shows Free PE/size. The value of this field should show space that is equal to or more than the additional space needed. You will need to extend the volume group by the amount of space required if there is insufficient space.

Extend The Logical Volume

You can use the lvextend command to extend the logical volume. You can pass the name of the logical volume device as an argument to the command.

[root@desktop~]# lvextend -L +400M /dev/vgone/zeus

This command will increase the space of the logical volume zeus by 400 MiB.

Extend The File System

The final step is to extend the file system. This is the only step that differs from the steps we used in extending an XFS file system.

You can use the resize2fs /dev/vgname/lvname command the extend the file system in the EXT4 file system. Just like in the case of xfs_growfs, even with this command, you can resize the file system while it is in a mounted state. You can also pass the -p option to the command if you wish to see the progress on the resizing operation.

[root@desktop~]# resize2fs /dev/vgone/zeus

Note: The main difference in the two command xfs_growfs and resize2fs is the argument that you pass for the identification of the file system. In the xfs_growfs, the argument that you pass is the mount point of the file system. While in the resize2fs command, the argument that you pass is the name of the logical volume.

CHAPTER 11

◆━┄━━━━━◆━┄━◆━┄━◆━━━━━━━━┄━◆

Troubleshooting Issues in the
Red Hat Enterprise Linux Boot Process

The goal of this chapter is to learn how to troubleshoot problems encountered during the boot process of Red Hat Enterprise Linux. We will study in detail about the boot process in Red Hat Enterprise Linux first and then learn how to fix common issues faced during the boot process. We will also learn how to fix the file system issues and problems related to the boot loader.

The Red Hat Enterprise Linux Boot Process

By the end of this section, you will learn about the Red Hat Enterprise Linux boot process and how to influence it.

The Boot Process

A complex combination of software and hardware results in the formation of modern computer systems. A system starts from a state without any power to running in a graphical mode which interacts with the user. For this to be possible, a large number of hardware and software pieces needs to run in harmony. This part of this chapter will give you a detailed description of how an x86_64 system goes through the booting process while running the Red Hat Enterprise Linux 7. Even if you are running an x86_64 virtual machine for Red Hat Enterprise Linux7, the boot process almost remains the same, except for the part that some hardware processes are taken care of by the software, which is the hypervisor. Let us go through the Red Hat Enterprise Linux 7 boot process step by step.

1. You power on the machine. The firmware of the system (which can be a modern UEFI or an older BIOS) will run a Power On Self Test called POST, and some of the hardware is initialized.

   Configured using: The BIOS or UEFI screens of the system are used to configure this. You can reach these screens by pressing a combination of keyboard keys such as F2 at the beginning of the boot process.

2. The firmware in the system will now search for a bootable device that is configured in the boot firmware like UEFI or BIOS, or it will search for the Master Boot Record MBR on all available disks. The search is performed by following an order that is defined in the BIOS.

   Configured using: The BIOS or UEFI screens of the system are used to configure this. You can reach these screens by pressing a combination of keyboard keys such as F2 at the beginning of the boot process.

3. In the next steps, the firmware in the system will read a boot loader from a disk, and the control of the system is then passed to the boot loader. The grub2 bootloader is typically used in Red Hat Enterprise Linux 7.

   Configured using: grub2-install

4. The configuration defined in the bootloader is loaded from the disk, and a menu of available boot configurations is presented to the user.

Configured using: /etc/grub.d/, /etc/default/grub and automatically through /boot/grub2/grub.cfg

5. The user can make a choice for the boot configuration to be loaded from the given menu, or it will be selected automatically after a defined timeout value. After the choice is made, the boot loader will load the selected kernel and initramfs from the disk and load them into the memory. Kernel modules for all the necessary hardware, required boot scripts, etc. to boot the system are located in initramfs, which is a gzip-ed cpio. A complete usable system is available in initramfs on the Red Hat Enterprise Linux 7.

   Configured using: /etc/dracut.conf

6. In the next step, the control of the system is passed to the kernel by the boot loader. While doing so, certain options may be passed to the kernel using the command line in the boot loader, one option being the location of initramfs in the memory.

   Configured using: /etc/grub.d/, /etc/default/grub and automatically through /boot/grub2/grub.cfg

7. The kernel will initialize all the hardware for which the drivers are available through initramfs. It then executes /sbin/init from initramfs as PID 1. There is a working copy of systemd as /sbin/init available on Red Hat Enterprise Linux 7. It is also available as a udev daemon.

   Configured using: init= command line parameter.

8. The control is taken over by the systemd instance from initramfs. It executes all units for the initrd.target target. This involves mounting the actual root file system on /sysroot.

   Configured using /etc/fstab

9. The kernel root file system is switched from the root file system of initramfs to the previously mounted system root file system, which was mounted on /sysroot.systemd. It then uses a copy of systemd installed on the system to re-execute itself.

10. In the last step, systemd looks for a default target. This default target can be passed through the kernel command line, or it is automatically configured on the system. Systemd then starts and stops units until they are compatible with the default target. While doing so, dependencies between units are solved automatically. In its essence, a systemd target is a collection of units that need to be activated so that the system can reach a specific state. These targets would include a graphical login screen or a text-based login screen for sure.

Configured using: /etc/systemd/system/default.target, /etc/systemd/system/

Boot, Reboot and Shut Down

1. The systemctl command can be used from the command line if a system admin wants to power off or reboot a system.

2. systemctl poweroff command will result in all services being stopped, all file systems being unmounted, and then powering off the system.

3. systemctl reboot command will result in all running services being stopped, all file systems being unmounted, and the system is rebooted.

To ensure that Red Hat Enterprise Linux 7 is backward compatible, the commands such as power off and reboot still work, but they are just symbolic links to the systemctl link.

Note: The commands such as systemctl halt and halt are also available to stop the system, but unlike poweroff, these commands do not power off the system. These commands only reduce the system to a point where it will be safe to switch off the system manually.

Selecting a Systemd Target

As already discussed, a systemd target is a collection of systemd units that need to be activated so that the system reached a desired state. Some of the most important systemd targets are listed in the table below.

target	purpose
graphical.target	Multiple users support Text-based logins and graphical logins.
multi-user.target	Multiple user logins are supported but only in the text-based login mode.
rescue.target	This is the **sulogin** prompt where the initialization for a basic system has been completed.
emergency.target	This is the **sulogin** prompt where initramfs pivot has been completed, and the system root is mounted on / read-only.

A target can be very much a part of another target, as well. For example, the multi-user.target is a subset of the graphical.target, which in turn is a part of the basic.target and others. You can use the following commands to view these dependencies on the command line.

[root@desktop~]# systemctl list-dependencies graphical.target | grep target

You can get an overview of all the targets using the following command.

[root@desktop~]# systemctl list-units --type=target --all

You can get an overview of all the targets installed on the disk using the following command.

[root@desktop~]# systemctl list-unit-files --type=target --all

Selecting a Target a Runtime

As a system administrator, you can select a different target for the system to load when the system is in runtime. The command to be used is systemctl isolate.

[root@desktop~]# systemctl isolate multi-user.target

When you isolate a target, services that are not required by that target and its dependencies are stopped. At the same time, it will start any required services that have not been started yet.

Note: It is not possible to isolate all targets. Only if targets have AllowIsolate-Yes configured in their system files, they can be isolated. For example, it is possible to isolate the graphical.target target, but you will not be able to isolate cryptsetup.target.

Setting a Default Target

When the system starts, systemd takes control of initramfs. systemd will then try to activate the default.target target. Mostly the default.target target is a symbolic link to either graphical.target or multi-user.target stored in /etc/systemd/system.

You do not need to edit this symbolic link manually as there are two tools available in systemctl to manage this link: get-default and set-default.

[root@desktop~]# systemctl get-default

multi-user.target

[root@desktop~]# systemctl set-default graphical.target

This will change the default target to graphical.target

[root@desktop~]# systemctl get-default

Graphical.target

Specifying a Different Target at Boot Time

You can pass a special option to the kernel command line during the boot time if you wish to specify a different target. The option is systemd.unit=

For example, if you wish to boot the system into rescue more so that you can make changes to the configuration when no services are running, you can append the following option to the kernel command line from the interactive boot loader menu.

systemd.unit=rescue.target

This change in the target configuration is effective only for that particular boot. It is useful when you need to troubleshoot issues related to the booting of the system.

You can select a different target at boot time in Red Hat Enterprise Linux 7 by following the steps given below.

- Start the system or reboot the system.

- When you reach the boot loader menu, you can interrupt the countdown by pressing any key.

- Take the cursor over to the entry to be started.

- Press e to edit the current entry.

- Take the cursor to the line that begins with linux16. This is the command line for the kernel.

- Pass the following command systemd.unit=required target.

- Press control+x to boot the system with these changes.

Troubleshooting Common Issues Encountered during Boot Time

After going through this section, you will be able to fix the common problems faced during boot time.

How to Recover the Root Password

One of the most essential things of a Linux system is the root system. So it is a fundamental task for a system admin to know how to recover the root password if it gets lost. This is a straightforward task if the system admin is already logged in as a root user or a sudo user with full privileges. This task becomes a little more complicated when the system admin is not logged into the system.

There are multiple methods to set a new root password. One of the methods is where you can boot the Linux system from a live USB, mount the root file system and then edit the password in the /etc/shadow file. In this section, we will be learning to use a method that does not need you to use any external media to recover the root password.

Note: If you were to use Red Hat Enterprise Linux version 6 or less, there was an option to boot the system in runlevel 1, where the system admin would be presented with the root prompt. The closest equivalent to runlevel 1 on the Red Hat Enterprise Linux 7 is the rescue.target or the emergency.target, and both would require you to know the root password to login.

Red Hat Enterprise Linux 7 gives you the option to pause the scripts that run from initramfs at specific points. It will also allow you to provide a root shell and continue with the root shell while it exists. This option is available mainly for debugging purposes, but you can also use it to recover the root password. Let us go through the steps involved in this process one by one.

- Reboot the system.

- When you reach the screen with the interactive boot loader countdown, interrupt the countdown by pressing any key.

- Take the cursor to the entry which you want to boot.

- Press e to edit the selected entry.

- This will take you to the kernel command line. Take the cursor to the line that starts with linux16.

- Append rd.break to this line. This will break the boot process before the control is passed to the actual system from initramfs.

- Press Ctrl+c to reboot the system with the changes.

When the system boots now, thanks to the rd.break command, you will be presented with a root shell, with the root file system of the actual system, which is mounted on /sysroot.

The next steps will help you recover the root passwords. Let's go through these steps one by one.

- You first need to remount /sysroot as a read and write file system. You can use the following command for it.

  switch_root:/# mount -oremount, rw /sysroot

- You will need to switch to the chroot jail as /sysroot is treated as the root of the file system in this jail.

  switch _root:/# chroot /sysroot

- In this step, you can set a new root password.

  sh-4.2# passwd root

- You need to pass the autorelabel command so that all unlabeled files get relabeled again during boot.

  sh-4.2# touch /.autorelabel

- You now need to type exit twice. The first exit will exit you from the chroot jail, and the second exit will exit you from the initramfs debug shell.

- Once this is done, the system will continue with the booting process followed by a complete SELinux relabel and then reboot the system again.

The journalctl Command

Looking at the logs of failed reboots can be useful too. If you have kept the journalctl log to run permanently, you can go through the logs using the journalctl tool.

The first thing to do is to ensure that journalctl logging has been enabled to run persistently.

```
[root@desktop~]# mkdir -p -m2775 /var/log/journal
```

```
[root@desktop~]# chown :systemd-journal /var/log/journal
```

```
[root@desktop~]# killall -USR1 systemd-journald
```

You can pass the -b option with the journalctl command if you want to see the logs of a previous boot. If you have not passed any arguments, -b option will make sure to display logs only about the current boot. If you pass a negative number as an argument, the logs will be filtered to show previous boots. Let us look at an example.

```
[root@desktop~]# journalctl -b-1 -p err
```

The output of this command will be all the messages that are flagged as an error or worse concerning the previous boot.

Diagnosing and Fixing systemd Boot Issues

If there are issues encountered when the services are starting up, there are a few tools that are available to system admins so that they can debug and troubleshoot the problem.

Early debug Shell

You can run the systemctl enable debug-shell.service command. This will spawn a root shell on TTY9 (which can be accessed using Ctrl+Alt+F9) during the early boot sequence. You will be automatically logged in as the root user on this shell, allowing you to use other available tools for debugging while the system is still in the boot process.

Note: It is crucial to turn off the debug-shell.service service after you are done using it. Otherwise, it will leave an unauthenticated root shell open, and anyone with access to the local console can access this shell.

Emergency and Rescue Targets

If you append systemd.unit=rescue.target or systemd.unit=emergency.target to the kernel command line from the boot loader menu, the system will spawn into a rescue shell or an emergency shell instead of a normal boot. It is essential to know the root password to use both of these shells. The root file system is mounted in the read-only mode in the emergency target shell, while in the rescue target shell, the hell will wait for sysinit.target to conclude so that more services of the system are initialized.

You can use both these shells to troubleshoot issues that are preventing the system from a normal boot. The problems can range from anything such as a dependency loop between service, to an incorrect entry in the /etc/fstab file. When you exit from these shells, the system will continue with the regular boot process.

Stuck Jobs

Multiple jobs are started by systemd during the startup process. There are chances that some of these jobs do not complete, and they further stop other jobs from completing too. As a system admin, you can use the command systemctl list-jobs command to see the current list of jobs. Jobs with the status running need to complete before jobs with the status waiting can continue.

Fixing Issues Related to the File System at Boot Time

After completing this section, you would be able to fix issues related to the file system during boot time.

A system may fail to boot if there are incorrect entries in the /etc/fstab file or if the file system has been corrupted. In most situations, systemd will continue with the boot process after a timeout, or it will direct the boot process to an emergency shell where the root password is required.

The following table will take you through some of the common errors and their results.

Problem	Result
The file system has been corrupted	Fsch will be attempted by systemd. If an automatic fix also does not solve the problem, you will be prompted to run fsck manually from an emergency shell.
There is a reference to a UUID that does not exist in the /etc/fstab file	systemd will wait for some time to see if the device becomes available. If the device does not become available, the user will be directed to an emergency shell after a specific timeout value.
There is a reference to a mount point that does not exist in the /etc/fstab file	systemd will try to create the mount point automatically. If it does not succeed, it will redirect the user to the emergency shell.
The option for mounting specified in the /etc/fstab file is incorrect	You will be redirected to the emergency shell without any other processes.

As a system admin, in all the above cases, you have the choice to use the emergency.target shell directly to understand and fix the problem, as no other files will be mounted before the emergency shell is displayed.

Note: If you are using the automatic recovery shell when you encounter file system issues, it is vital to use the systemctl daemon-reload command after you edit the entries in the /etc/fstab file. Without reloading, systemd will continue using the older versions of the /etc/fstab file.

Fixing Issues Faced with the Boot Loader

After completing this section, you would be able to fix the common problems encountered with the boot loader.

The default boot loader used by Red Hat Enterprise Linux 7 is known as grub2. GRUB stands for Grand Unified Bootloader, and grub2 is the second version of it.

Both UEFI and BIOS support the grub2, and grub2 also supports booting any operating system that works well with modern hardware.

The main configuration file for grub2 is located at /boot/grub2/grub.cfg. However, as a system admin, it is not advisable to edit this main file directly. Instead, there is a tool available to make changes to the grub configuration as required. The tool is known as grub2-mkconfig, and it makes use of various configuration files and installed kernels to make changes to the grub2 configuration.

The grub2-mkconfig tool looks at the file at /etc/default/grub to edit the options just as the kernel command line to be used, and the default timeout of each menu. Once this has been established, the tool uses scripts located at /etc/grub.d/ to create a configuration file for grub2.

If you wish to make permanent changes to the boot loader configuration, you will need to edit the previously listed configuration file, followed by the command given below.

[root@desktop~]# grub2-mkconfig > /boot/grub2/grub.cfg

If you have created major changes to the configuration as a system admin, you may want to run the above command without any redirection so that you can see the output of the command in real-time.

Important Directives

It is crucial for you as a system admin to know the syntax of the file at /boot/grub2/grub.cfg if you want to troubleshoot a broken configuration in grub2. The actual entries of the bootable code are encoded inside the menuentry blocks. Inside these entries, the lines which contain linux16 and initrd16 point to the kernel that is to be used from the disk(in addition to the kernel command line). It also points to the initramfs that is to be loaded. You can use tab completion to find the lines containing these entries when you are on the interactive editing boot menu.

The set root line does not point to the root file system of Red Hat Enterprise Linux 7. It will instead point to the file system from where grub2 is expected to load initramfs and kernel files. The syntax is hard drive-partition where hd0 is the first hard disk in the system, hd1 is the second hard disk in the system, and so on. If there is an MBR partition, it is indicated as msdos1, while a GPT partition is indicated as gpt1.

Reinstalling the Boot Loader

If you come across a case where the boot loader itself got corrupted, you can use the grub2-install command to reinstall it. You will need to provide MBR of the disk as an argument if you are using a BIOS system. On UEFI systems, you will not need to pass any arguments as the EFI system partition is already mounted at /boot/efi.

Conclusion

A s you know, we have progressed and learned a lot about the Linux operating system and the profile of a Linux System Administrator. There are plenty of opportunities for a system administrator in the world, and we hope that this book will motivate you to become better and better at it.

This book takes into consideration the Red Hat Enterprise Linux 7 operating system that is the operating system of choice for almost all the organizations in the world to run their servers. Even if they use a different operating system, the syntax of all the commands that you have learned in this book will only be marginally different from Red Hat Enterprise Linux 7.

As much as you have learned in this book, the journey to becoming a great system administrator has just begun, and there are still miles to go so that you can perfect it. We will hope that we can motivate you as much as we can through our books on Linux Administration.

References

https://www.redhat.com/en/services/training/rh134-red-hat-system-administration-ii

https://github.com/konduruvijaykumar/LINUX-GUIDE/blob/master/Red%20Hat%20System%20Administration%20II%20RH134%20%20Geekboy.ir%20.pdf

www.ingramcontent.com/pod-product-compliance
Lightning Source LLC
Chambersburg PA
CBHW071252050326
40690CB00011B/2359